OTABIND®

INTERNATIONAL

W9-ATZ-354

Dear Friend:

You may have noticed that this book is put together differently than most other quality paperbacks. The page you are reading, for instance, along with the back page, is glued to the cover. And when you open the book the spine "floats" in back of the pages. But there's nothing wrong with your book. These features allow us to produce what is known as a detached cover, specifically designed to prevent the spine from cracking even after repeated use. A state-of-the-art binding technology known as OtaBind® is used in the manufacturing of this and all Health Communications, Inc. books.

HCI has invested in equipment and resources that ensure the books we produce are of the highest quality, yet remain affordable. At our Deerfield Beach headquarters, our editorial and art departments are just a few steps from our pressroom, bindery and shipping facilities. This internal production enables us to pay special attention to the needs of our readers when we create our books.

Our titles are written to help you improve the quality of your life. You may find yourself referring to this book repeatedly, and you may want to share it with family and friends who can also benefit from the information it contains. For these reasons, our books have to be durable and, more importantly, user-friendly.

OtaBind® gives us these qualities. Along with a crease-free spine, the book you have in your hands has some other characteristics you may not be aware of:

• Open the book to any page and it will lie flat, so you'll never have to worry about losing your place.

• You can bend the book over backwards without damage, allowing you to hold it with one hand.

• The spine is 3-5 times stronger than conventional perfect binding, preventing damage even with rough handling.

This all adds up to a better product for our readers—one that will last for years to come. We stand behind the quality of our books and guarantee that, if you're not completely satisfied, we'll replace the book or refund your money within 30 days of purchase. If you have any questions about this guarantee or our bookbinding process, please feel free to contact our customer service department at 1-800-851-9100.

We hope you enjoy the quality of this book, and find understanding, insight and direction for your life in the information it provides.

Health Communications, Inc.®

3201 S.W. 15th Street
Deerfield Beach, FL 33442-8190
(305) 360-0909

Peter Vegso
President

Comments on the Writing and Artwork of Sri Chinmoy

On Sri Chinmoy's Poems and Stories:

"U.N. delegates and staff members should read the deep spiritual insights of the United Nations' guru, Sri Chinmoy. The young people who are looking to oriental sages and spiritual seers for enlightenment should also turn to him who has come from India to interpret the spiritual journey of the United Nations."

Dr. Robert Müller
Former Assistant Secretary-General of the United Nations;
Chancellor, University for Peace

"The poems are beautiful in their simplicity and profound in their significance."

Professor Ralph Lazzaro
Director of Language Studies, Harvard Divinity School

"Sri Chinmoy is India's eloquent cultural ambassador and a priceless gift to the West. His writings have the amazing capacity of ennobling our thoughts, quickening our spirit and inspiring us to strive toward self-realization."

S. Ramakrishnan
Director General, Bharatiya Vidya Bhavan (International)

"Your paintings convey many messages of our deepest spiritual nature, as do your poetry, your biographical sketches of the great men of your time and your words of inspiration with which you encouraged the late President Ranasinghe Premadasa of my country, and even people with much greater responsibilities, like Mikhail Gorbachev. You are one of the rarest gifts that humankind of the 21st century has."

Ambassador Dr. Ananda W.P. Guruge
Ambassador of Sri Lanka to the United States

". . . a captivating saga of enchanting poetry and beautiful music reflecting your humanistic nature and your inexhaustible efforts at attaining peace for all peoples."

Ambassador Aleksandr Razvin
Deputy Permanent Representative of Russia to the United Nations

"In the present day, undoubtedly the greatest innovator in the language is Sri Chinmoy. The rich and revealing parallel structure, the fusion of nouns into compounds, and the use of rhetorical paradigms together create what might have been thought impossible in the English language—the effect of word-shrines."

Dr. Meredith Bennett
from *Simplicity and Power: The Poetry of Sri Chinmoy*

"Sri Chinmoy is the foremost mystic and spiritual poet of the 20th century."

Dr. P. Jayaraman
Executive Director, Bharatiya Vidya Bhavan, USA

On Sri Chinmoy's
Million Soul Bird Illustrations:

"These soul birds, symbols of freedom, joy and love, will undoubtedly inspire countless individuals and remain as a lasting tribute to peace and harmony."

Rt. Hon. Jean Chrétien
Prime Minister of Canada

"May such a mammoth and magnificent achievement be an inspiration to all of us working for peace worldwide."

Rt. Hon. James Bolger
Prime Minister of New Zealand

"Your million birds will be an inspiration to everyone to continue to work for our common goal of peace—peace in our lives and communities, and peace on earth."

Dr. Linus Pauling
Nobel Laureate in Peace (1962) and in Chemistry (1954)

"Congratulations on your million bird drawings. Their beauty inspires us all. To finish 1 million birds in the outer world transmits a powerful message for all of us to keep our hearts open to the great and peaceful inner world."

Sudahota Carl Lewis
Eight-time Olympic Gold Medalist in Track and Field

Garden
OF THE Soul

*Lessons on Living
in Peace, Happiness
and Harmony*

Sri Chinmoy

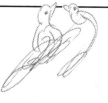

Health Communications, Inc.
Deerfield Beach, Florida

Library of Congress Cataloging-in-Publication Data
Chinmoy, Sri

    Garden of the soul: lessons on living in peace, happiness
and harmony / Sri Chinmoy.
    p.   cm.
    ISBN 1-55874-314-6 (pbk.): $9.95
    1. Spiritual life.   2. Parables.   3. Meditations.   I. Title.
BL624.2.C48 1994   94-23026
294.5'43—dc20   CIP

©1994 Sri Chinmoy
ISBN 1-55874-314-6

Publisher: Health Communications, Inc.
              3201 S.W. 15th Street
              Deerfield Beach, Florida 33442-8190

Cover design by Lawna P. Oldfield

Contents

Introduction

Inside each of us there is a beautiful flower garden. This is the garden of the soul. Here we can enjoy the fragrance of each and every flower and discover the true beauty and boundless freedom of our inner selves. With every lesson we learn from life, our soul-garden grows and glows. Ultimately, the peace, light and happiness-fragrance of our individual gardens will spread throughout the length and breadth of the world.

The lessons presented in this book are simple, yet they speak eternal truths: love God and serve Him inside humanity; seek inner peace; cultivate simplicity, sincerity, purity and humility; still the restless mind; expand the heart. Many are stories from India's ancient past, others relate episodes in the lives of some of humanity's great figures. I feel that these wise lessons from the East are timeless and truly universal. It is with great love that I share them with readers in the West.

When we expand ourselves, we feel that our whole existence has become like a divine bird that soars into the Beyond. While flying in this realm of delight, we are not bound by any limitations. We are free from the meshes of ignorance and our wings are widespread with peace, joy and love. At the beginning of each story, I return to the birds and their special message. May these sunrise-birds take flight in your heart.

—*Sri Chinmoy*

*In tomorrow's world
Many things will
enlighten humanity.
But the thing that will enlighten
Humanity's inner and
outer life most
Is the transcendental temple
Of universal silence.*

Silence Liberates

There lived a pious man in Bengal, India. Every day a Sanskrit scholar would come to his house and read aloud a few soul-stirring spiritual teachings from the Gita, the Upanishads and the Vedas. The master of the house listened devotedly to these discourses.

The family had a bird called Krishna. It was kept in a cage in the room where the discourses were given and also listened to these talks.

One day the bird spoke to its master and said, "Could you please tell me what benefit you derive from these spiritual talks?"

The master answered, "Krishna, you don't seem to understand that these spiritual talks will liberate me, free me from bondage!"

The bird said, "You have been listening to these discourses for the last few years, but I don't see any changes in you. Would you kindly ask your teacher what will actually happen to you?"

On the following day the master of the house said to his teacher, "Guru, I have been listening to your spiritual talks for the last 10 years. Is it true that I will get liberation and freedom?"

The teacher was still. He scratched his head, pondered the question, but found no reply. He remained silent for about an hour and then left the house.

The master of the house was stunned. His guru could not give an answer to the bird's question, but the bird found an answer.

From that day on, the bird stopped eating. It stopped singing. It became absolutely silent. The master and his family placed food inside the cage every day, but the bird would not touch anything.

One day the master looked at the bird and, seeing no sign of life in it, took it gently out of the cage. With a sad heart, he placed his Krishna on the floor. In a twinkling, the bird flew away into the infinite freedom of the sky!

The bird taught. Its master and his guru learned: silence liberates.

*I may at most begin
the journey;
God's boundless Bounty
Will have to complete
My heavenward progress-life.*

Safe in the Master's Compassionate Concern

A sincere seeker was looking for a Guru. The poor man had spent years searching, but had found no Guru who really pleased him. He had met many spiritual Masters, but he did not care for any of them. Now he was miserable, for he felt that his days were passing in vain.

One night he had a dream. In his dream he came to know who his Guru was, and the following morning he set out for his Guru's house, which was about 16 miles from his own.

Since the Guru lived in one village and he lived in another, he had no choice but to walk. It was early morning, and everything was calm and quiet. He felt immensely happy and excited. He did not actually know where his Guru's village was, but he thought that he would be able to ask directions of the people he passed and reach his destination that way. Once there, he knew he would recognize the house.

The seeker walked for about six miles until he came to a large crossroad; he was not sure which route to take. Looking around for someone to ask for directions, he saw a young woman fetching water from a pond by the crossing. She had a pitcher with her, and she filled it to the brim. Then she started carrying it down the road that led to the north. When the seeker saw the beauty of the woman, he felt compelled to follow her, and this made him sad and angry with himself.

He thought, "Now my journey will be all in vain! Temptation has already caught me. This stupid woman has ruined all my aspiration. She is a curse! O God, now where is my Guru, where is my goal? She has ruined me. I have read the books of spiritual Masters. They all say that women will take us to hell. At last I am going to find my Guru, and she has to be right in front of me!"

So he cursed the woman inwardly. But she was not paying any attention to him. She walked along the road, full of joy and purity. The man continued to follow her. What else could he do? He could either go home or continue on that road until he met a man to ask. He decided to walk on, following the woman, and thought to himself, "What is wrong with her? Why is she carrying such a big pitcher along this road for such a long way, always ahead of me?"

After traveling about four miles in this unfortunate state, he came to another intersection. There the seeker saw a little boy, naked, playing in the street and singing a village song:

To the north is the goal.
To the south is breath.
To the east is destruction.
To the west is frustration.

The man could not understand the meaning of the words, and he wondered why the child was singing so soulfully. But he decided to continue following the road on which the child was playing, and he went on his way while the child kept singing.

As he walked away listening to the child's song, he became aware that the woman with the pitcher had disappeared. She was nowhere to be seen. He was relieved and happy that she had left him, for he had been sorely tempted by her beauty.

The seeker walked for another five or six miles, and again he began to wonder where he was and whether he would ever be able to find his Guru's house. Tremendous doubt entered his mind. What could he do? It was very strange–on other days there would have been some people on the road, but today there were none. Finally he said to himself, "All right, let me walk on for another mile or so. Then if I don't find anyone, I shall return home."

After covering a mile, the seeker entered a village. Still uncertain whether he was on the right road, he was about to turn back when he again saw the woman with the pitcher. She was looking at him with great compassion, but he became very angry. "Again you have come to tempt me!" he cried. "Just a few hours ago you left me in peace, and now you have come again!"

He was very angry, but the woman just pointed to a particular house. The seeker went to the house and there inside he saw his spiritual Master. He was flooded with joy and he touched his Master's feet and was blessed by the Master.

After they had talked and meditated together for a few hours, the Master said to the disciple, "Now come, let us go and see my fields. I have a large vegetable garden." The new disciple was delighted to go with his Master.

While they were in the field, they saw a neighbor taking away two eggplants without permission. The Master flew into a rage. "How dare you do this without asking!" he shouted.

The neighbor said, "My wife has no food to cook. Because you are a spiritual man, I knew you would not miss these eggplants. I am taking only two."

The Master said, "No, you can't do that. You are taking them without my permission!" A terrible quarrel ensued. The Master threatened to strike his neighbor.

The new disciple wondered, "O God, what kind of Master is this?"

At last the Master said, "All right, take them. I don't need them. You take the two eggplants." Then he said to the disciple, "Let us go home."

The disciple and the Master went back and had their supper. Then the Master said, "Let us meditate."

But the disciple could not meditate at all. He kept remembering the Master's anger, and thought, "The Master is so mean, he cannot even give his neighbor two eggplants." He was very upset and unhappy and thought, "I was mistaken. This man cannot be my Master. He is so cruel. He is so unkind. Tomorrow, early in the morning before he gets up, I will leave without his knowledge."

So in the small hours of the morning, while the Master was still fast asleep, the disciple tiptoed out of the Master's house.

As he stood outside about to run away, he again saw the beautiful woman who the day before had carried the pitcher of water. She asked him to carry a bag for her, and he felt compelled to take it. As soon as he had it in his hands, the woman began shouting, "Thief, thief, thief!"

The Master woke up when he heard the shouting and ran out of his house, catching the man by the arm. Then he saw that it was his new disciple. When he opened the bag, he discovered that there were two eggplants inside.

The Master said to the disciple, "You thief, did you take these eggplants yesterday? You certainly didn't take them this morning. Or perhaps you entered into my storage barn and stole them."

The disciple protested, "I didn't steal them! This woman insisted that I take them, and I could not resist. I don't know what kind of charm she has, but she put them into my hand and I couldn't seem to throw them away. And then she cried out, 'Thief, thief!' But this is a false accusation. She is the thief; I am not." He wanted to hit the woman right then and there, but when he was about to strike her she disappeared.

"Master, please tell me who this woman is," cried the astonished disciple. "Why does she make problems for me all the time? I didn't tell you, but yesterday she nearly ruined my journey at the very beginning. I started out to find you, full of eagerness, enthusiasm and joy. But soon after I set out, I saw her fetching water. She tempted me. Her beauty disturbed me. She walked ahead of me for a long way before she disappeared. Later I saw her near your door, and again this morning. Master, save me from this woman!"

The Master said, "Why did you try to leave me?"

The disciple answered, "O Master, what could I think of you? You were insulting that man about two eggplants. How can a spiritual Master be so mean?"

The Master said, "It was not meanness. If that man had asked my permission, I would gladly have given him as many eggplants as he wanted. But if he does not ask my permission, then he is stealing. Forgiveness is always there: you saw that I forgave him for taking those two eggplants. But if he does this without my permission, today he will take two, tomorrow twenty, and the day after tomorrow he will take everything I have."

He continued, "Like me, you grow fruits and vegetables in your garden. I know that your neighbors take away your things and your wife gets angry about it. But you say,

'O, don't worry, it is not a serious matter. After all, we are all God's children; it is all God's property. Who cares?' And you suffer financially afterwards. You are expected to sell fruits for your livelihood, but you let your neighbors steal so much that your wife can't make ends meet. You are making a serious mistake. Your neighbors will remain lazy, and they will become real thieves.

"I did this to show you that you are doing the wrong thing. The thief was not my neighbor; it was me. I can take any form. I quarreled and fought with myself only to show you that stealing is something you must not encourage. Nobody should take another's possessions without his knowledge, approval and permission."

The seeker said, "Forgive me, Master. I wish to continue as your disciple. But what about that stupid woman? You know I was so pure, so spiritual. Why has she bothered and tempted me?"

With a broad smile the Master said, "That beautiful woman was also me."

"Why did you do that?" asked the disciple.

"Look here," said the Master. "The first time you saw her, you were feeling totally lost. You did not know your way, and there was nobody there to guide you. I took the form of a beautiful woman because I knew that you still had vital desire within you that you hadn't fully conquered. She was absolutely pure, but you felt lustful toward her. You cursed her. That is what men do when they see a woman. Inwardly they desire her, and outwardly they curse her. They say, 'She has ruined me.' But she did not ruin you. You ruined yourself by inwardly throwing all your own impurities onto her.

"I wanted you to come to my house, but how? I had to bring you myself, since there was nobody else around. It was the beauty of the woman that brought you to the child. You covered the distance because you appreciated and admired her beauty. If it had been somebody else, say some man, you would have doubted him. You would have been unsure; you would have said, 'Perhaps he does not know the way.' But you followed this woman spontaneously. Her beauty compelled you to go on. Her love was absolutely pure and divine. Her concern for you was supremely genuine."

"Why then did she leave me when I saw the little boy?"

"That little boy was also me. You were cursing the girl, and at the same time following her. I said, 'Now let me use some other means and give him some relief.' I got the idea of assuming another form, that of a child. He was innocent and pure. He sang so soulfully. You were tempted by the beautiful woman, but you had no physical attraction for the boy. The boy had a greater advantage. He was so innocent. He was like nature–absolutely pure."

"But why was the boy singing?" asked the disciple. "The song seemed so meaningless to me: 'To the north is the goal, to the south is breath, to the east is destruction, to the west is frustration.' What does it mean?"

The Master replied, "I was singing through that boy. 'To the north is the goal. . . .' You see, you followed my instructions unconsciously. To the north was my house. 'To the south is breath. . . .' Breath is rest; breath is your own home. You did not go back toward the south. When you return home, you will get rest. And if you had followed the road that was leading toward the east, it would have meant destruction because there were two *dacoits* [armed robbers] there. Whoever went along the road toward the east from the place where the boy was would have been attacked by highway robbers. First they would have searched you, and if you had not had enough money, they would have taken much pleasure in killing you. If you had followed the road to the west, you would have found only frustration because there was no goal there. This is the meaning of the song. Unconsciously you followed the child's message. You walked toward the north and reached your destination."

"O Master, my Master!" cried the disciple. Then he asked, "But why did that woman come to bother me again?"

The Master replied, "Again, the woman was me. I assumed another form. After walking a few miles, you got lost again. You were confused, you were hesitating, you were ready to turn back. I took that form and, full of compassion, showed you my own home."

"But was it necessary to do all this?" asked the disciple.

"Yes, it was necessary," replied the Master. "You needed to learn that if purity is not fully established when you run toward your Master, towards your Goal, then you should run with impurity. There is no harm if you cannot walk along the path with absolute purity, especially in the beginning. Walk toward the Goal even with impurity. Your impurity will eventually be transformed.

"Then, you see, if you have childlike innocence, you will find joy. You started with impurity. With an innocent feeling and spontaneous inner joy you can go farther. When you go still farther, you will be inundated with divine compassion."

The seeker touched his Master's feet, saying, "Master, now I understand. You have helped me; you are truly my Master."

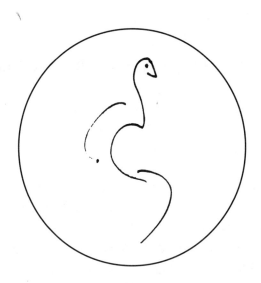

Do not allow yourself
To be ruled by dark doubts.
Make friends with bright hopes
At every moment
To change your own world
And the world around you.

This Plant Is Man, This Plant Is God

There was a seeker who for many years had been searching for a Master, a Guru, to guide him. He had visited many spiritual groups, but the teachers he met were not to his liking, so he continued searching. One day while he was walking along the street, he saw a spiritual Master with a few disciples. They were sitting on a beautiful lawn. Some of the disciples were watering the grass.

This seeker approached the Master and said, "Master, all these disciples of yours listen to you no matter what you say. They believe in you and they are right when they listen to you. But I have something to tell you, even though you will not see eye-to-eye with me."

The Master said, "Truth is certainly not my monopoly. If you have discovered some truth, I will accept it. Now please tell me, what is the truth that you have discovered?"

So the seeker said, "My discovery is this: a worldly person cannot easily realize God. I am a worldly human being, and I know that even to get a Master is simply impossible. I haven't found a spiritual teacher, for no spiritual teacher is satisfactory to me; so how will it be possible for me to realize God, which is infinitely more difficult? If finding a Master is so difficult for me, then finding spiritual realization in this life is simply impossible. Do you agree with me?"

The Master replied, "I don't agree. Others may think that what you say is right, but it is not difficult to find a Master or to find God."

The seeker was surprised, and even the disciples were to some extent amazed at the Master's remark because most of them knew how hard it had been for them to find a spiritual Master, and finding God-realization was still far beyond their imagination.

The Master said, "Look here. Right now some of my disciples are watering the grass. There are tiny plants everywhere." The Master pointed out two very tiny plants. Then the Master took a gardening tool and dug up one of them. Taking both the root and the leaf, the whole plant, he went to another plant. There he dug up the second plant and replaced it with the first one. Then he placed the second plant where the first one had been.

Then the Master said, "This plant is man, and this plant is God. I am a Master. I touched this plant, and as soon as I touched it, the plant gave me the divine response; then I took it and put it where the plant called 'God' had been. Then I put the God-plant, with all His compassion, love, joy and delight where the man-plant had been. It was a matter of only a few minutes. I took man to God and brought God to man."

The new seeker said, "Master, I wish to be your disciple. Please initiate me."

"I shall initiate you shortly, my child," the Master said. Then he continued, "If you feel that it is next to impossible to realize God, it means that your idea of God is wrong, your idea of spirituality is wrong. You are attached to the world, but if you had the same attachment to God you would see that you can easily reach God. Now when I go to God, I knock at the door. Immediately He opens it and comes to me. I say, 'Please come with me.' He comes with His infinite Love, Joy, Blessings and Compassion. Then I come and knock at your door, but when I knock at your door you don't open it. You keep your door closed, bolted. Naturally God and I go back. Then when I want to take you to God's Palace, I say to you, 'You come with me.' When I knock at God's door again, God says that as you didn't open your door when I brought Him to you, He will not open His door to you. If you had opened your door when I brought God as the Guest, and if you had allowed Him to come in, naturally He would also have allowed you to come into His Palace. So if you keep your heart's door open, God can enter.

"But when I approach you, you are immediately disturbed. You think you have fear, doubt, vital emotional problems, jealousy and so forth. You don't want to expose yourself; you want to hide. But this plant that I moved, man the plant, showed no fear, no doubt, no shyness when I touched it–absolutely nothing. It was not at all afraid of its own ignorance. It was thrilled that somebody was taking it to another place which was God. So when a spiritual Master meditates on you or blesses you, at that time if you offer your ignorance and your imperfections along with your devoted qualities, then it is easy for the Master to guide you to God. If not, it is next to impossible for the Master to do anything to transform the consciousness of the disciples or even to purify their consciousness. It is only an exchange of two plants. This is what the Master does when he deals with his spiritual children. One plant is God, another plant is man."

Then the Master slowly walked away.

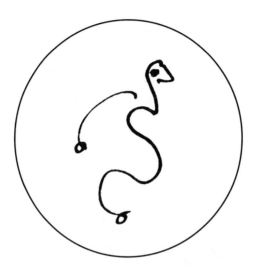

*Just start your inner race
Without waiting to see
Who else is ready to
run with you.
When others see you have
reached your goal,
They will also be
inspired to run.*

Go Alone

There was a great spiritual Master who quite often made predictions to his disciples. His predictions were not only good and inspiring, but also came true. Because of his many faultless predictions he became very well known in his country.

There came a time when this Master took a vow of silence, and for months did not speak at all. During this time he only wrote what he wanted to say to his disciples and friends. Any instructions he had to offer would be in writing.

One evening, two seekers who were friends came to visit the Master from a distant village. One of them was merely a curiosity-monger with no sincere aspiration; the other was indeed sincere. It happened that they arrived at a time when the Master had made a second vow, to keep his eyes closed in addition to remaining silent. They did not know of the Master's second vow until they arrived at his ashram.

When they approached the Master they saw a big queue of seekers. One by one they approached the Master, who was seated in silence with his eyes closed. Some of his close disciples stood by him. Each seeker was allowed to see the Master for only two or three seconds, and then the disciples standing by his side would signal them to leave.

A few hundred seekers stood on line ahead of these two particular seekers, these two close friends. All had their turn. The Master neither opened his eyes nor said a word to any of them. But when these two came and stood in front of him, he immediately opened his eyes.

His close disciples were very surprised. They said to themselves, "The Master has broken his promise to keep his eyes closed." Then, to their utter astonishment, he also broke his vow of silence. He said to the two seeker-friends, "Go alone. Go alone. Go alone."

The amazed attendants indicated that the two seekers' time was over. The two friends left the Master, and immediately he closed his eyes and resumed his silence. Now many more seekers came to the Master for his silent blessing, and left. The curiosity-monger was laughing hilariously as they started back. He said to his friend, "What kind of teacher is he? He was supposed to be silent and keep his eyes closed, but he opened his eyes and he spoke to us. He has broken both of his own promises."

Then the curiosity-monger became very angry with the Master. He said, "We have been lifelong friends. Now why does he ask us to 'go alone, go alone?' He wants to break up our friendship. He is cruel. I will never go to him again. You know that I would give my life for you, and I am sure that you would do the same for me. We are willing to make any sacrifice for each other, yet he wants our separation. We will always stay together."

It was evening as they made their way home, and they decided to take a short-cut. On their way they came to a shaky, delicate bamboo bridge. As the two were such very close friends, they decided to go together, one behind the other. As they walked onto the little bridge together it trembled and seemed about to collapse. It was so tiny and narrow that it could not hold two persons at a time. They saw a farmer near the bridge who cried out to them,

"Gentlemen, you are both wise. What are you doing? It isn't safe for you like that. Please cross the bridge one by one. Go alone. If you go alone this bridge will not collapse." The curiosity-monger would not move. He said jokingly, "Now we have another Yogi here. About an hour ago one Yogi said, 'Go alone', and now this farmer-Yogi is asking us to go alone."

Then he turned to the farmer and said, "Listen, it is none of your business. We are the closest of friends. We will go together even if we break our legs and our heads. You fool! We would rather die together than go alone. We will not allow ourselves to be separated. No, not even death can separate us."

The sincere seeker suddenly felt unsure. What should he do? Because of the strength of their friendship, his companion was saying that even if they were to break their legs, even if they were to die, they would not be separated, even for something as simple as crossing this little bridge.

The curiosity-monger continued to insult and abuse the farmer who had given them the advice to go alone. But the farmer said, "You can scold me, you can insult me, you can do anything you want. But I wish to tell you a few things. If you cross this bridge one by one, alone, it will take only a few minutes. When you are safely on the other side, then you can go on again with your closeness and friendship. You can give all your warmth, all your concern to each other. Why do you want to embrace death when you can escape it? Cross over separately, and then you can resume your closeness, your inseparable oneness. Why don't you use your wisdom?"

The curiosity-monger became furious. He was ready to strike the farmer. He shouted, "Go away or I'll crack your skull! I don't need your precious advice. I want to be with my friend all the time. If we die, we die together. We don't want your wise counsel. We went to see a Yogi and he told us to go alone. Now he has ruined all my inspiration and aspirations. Now you, farmer, you have become another Yogi. You are saying the same thing. I don't need you. Off with you!"

All the while something was happening inside the heart of the sincere seeker; he perceived something divine in the farmer. While he watched, fascinated, he saw the farmer's eyes reveal the depths of the vast blue sky. "Please give me more advice," he asked the farmer with utmost sincerity.

But the curiosity-monger simply wanted to make fun of the farmer. He said mockingly, "Yes, we need your advice. Go on."

The farmer turned to the curiosity-monger and said, "Both of you are spiritual seekers. You know that in the spiritual life all should go together, and you two wanted to go together. But what happens when one is tired, when one is unwilling to go farther? The one that is stronger and more competent should go on. He should continue to walk along the road to reach the goal, and bring back light, peace and bliss to offer to the one who is tired or reluctant to go farther. In order to inspire others more powerfully and convincingly, one has to go farther and get more inspiration, more light from the Golden Beyond.

"The two of you are one, but at the same time I see that *you* are only curious about the spiritual life, while *he* is serious and sincere. Under these circumstances you cannot go together. If he waits for you indefinitely, his spiritual life will be ruined. He will waste his precious time. And if you stay with someone who is in the spiritual life, and who is all aspiration while you are all curiosity, you will not benefit from him. Your curiosity will not draw any of his spiritual qualities. So you will also waste your precious time by staying with him.

"You should go on with your own life. Right now you are not ready for the spiritual life. You are just curious. You should follow your ordinary life. There you will get your own type of satisfaction by staying with your children, with the members of your family, with your friends and neighbors. Although it is not divine satisfaction–far from it–you will get some satisfaction by-mixing with people on your own level. And your friend will have real satisfaction by mixing with sincere seekers on his own level.

"If you two go alone, *you* will have satisfaction at your earthly level, and *he* will have satisfaction according to his spiritual needs. So go alone. Go alone. Go alone."

When the farmer said "Go alone" for the third time, his face changed into the face of the Yogi who had told them to go alone.

The sincere seeker touched the feet of the farmer, who was really the Yogi. But the curiosity-monger said, "You have ruined our friendship. You have ruined my life." And in his anger he struck the Teacher with all his might.

In return, the Master gave him a broad smile. He compassionately said, "You have given me a blow, but from now on you will be doing the right thing. That is why I am happy with you. I am sure that you will be following the right path according to your present needs."

To the sincere seeker he said, "I am proud of you. You are ready to follow the spiritual life. You will be following the right path, the spiritual path, your soul's own path. You have truly pleased me.

"Both of you have pleased me–each in his own way. Go alone. Go alone. Go alone."

*Beauty born of God's
Compassion-Light
Feeds the lost human beings
And encourages the awakened
human beings.*

A Compassionate Heart

Gambhirananda was a man of few words. People often misunderstood him, thinking him indifferent to the world, because he hid his compassionate heart. But when necessity demanded, he helped people, cured them and illumined them unreservedly and unconditionally.

Gambhirananda was fond of animals–both ferocious ones and tame household pets. Ferocious animals even roamed among the Master's attendants. These animals were very fond of Gambhirananda, and he gave them much affection and love.

One night, a disciple was sleeping outside the Master's room when a noise from inside the room woke him up. He quietly opened the door and saw the Master feeding quite a few mice small pieces of bread. He offered them the bread with great affection.

Gambhirananda was a little embarrassed to be seen feeding mice at that hour, but the disciple was very moved. The Master quite often showed tremendous indifference to seekers outwardly, but here the disciple saw that his compassionate heart cried even for poor little mice.

Commentary:

It is almost impossible to fathom a spiritual Master's compassion and sense of justice. His justice is admired and adored by the brave. His compassion is loved and adored by the hopeless and helpless. But his compassion and justice together prepare the seeker for an integrated understanding of God the Creator Supreme and God the creation manifested.

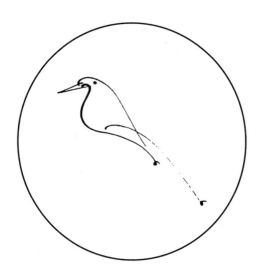

Now that you see through
Your real weakness,
Volcano-pride,
You are ready to discover
Your real strength,
Oneness-love.

The Scholar's Four Questions

There was once a great scholar. Everybody in the kingdom appreciated him because he was so learned. Unfortunately, in spite of his great learning he had great pride.

One day this scholar put on a gold necklace and went to the palace of another king. He said, "Whoever can defeat me in wisdom will get this necklace. I challenge everybody!"

All the scholars in that particular kingdom had heard about this scholar and they were afraid that they would lose. So they would not accept his challenge. The king was very sad that nobody would accept the challenge.

Finally, the court jester said, "I accept your challenge."

The king had almost surrendered to the scholar but thought it would be amusing to see his jester compete. He believed he was only a joker and would not be able to win the necklace.

The court jester said, "I will ask you four questions. If you answer any of my questions correctly, then you will lose, but if all your answers are incorrect, then I will accept defeat and the king will give you anything you want."

Then the court jester asked his first question: "Where do you come from?"

The scholar said, "I live here." This was incorrect, since he came from another kingdom. So by giving the wrong answer the scholar passed the first test.

The jester's second question was, "How long have you been here?"

"Three years," the scholar said, which was also incorrect. Still the court jester was unable to trick him.

The third time the jester asked, "Our king is good, kind and generous. Do you agree?"

The scholar said, "Your king? What you are saying is totally wrong. Your king is undivine and very unkind." So again the scholar passed the test.

The court jester said, "It seems that I can't defeat you. How many questions have I asked so far?"

The scholar said, "You have asked me three questions; you have one more. If I do not answer it correctly you will lose."

The court jester cried out, "Look! The scholar has lost. He has answered this question correctly."

So the scholar gave his necklace to the court jester, and the jester immediately gave it to the king. The scholar's pride was totally smashed. He said, "I will never come to your kingdom to challenge anybody again."

All the scholars were very impressed by the court jester's cleverness. They knew that they would not have been able to defeat the great scholar. The jester said, "You see, when great scholars are not alert, they lose. Had he been alert, he could have saved himself."

Love is the secret of oneness.
Sacrifice is the strength
of oneness.

The Gods Gain Immortality

Ᏸrihaspati is the Guru of the gods and Sukaracharya is the Guru of the demons. Brihaspati's and Sukaracharya's disciples often used to fight. At that time Sukaracharya had a special power that Brihaspati did not have. Sukaracharya knew a particular mantra that could bring his soldiers back to life after they had been killed on the battlefield. The cosmic gods felt miserable that Brihaspati did not have that capacity. In other ways–in wisdom, compassion and forgiveness–Brihaspati was far superior to Sukaracharya. In wisdom-light he was superior to everybody. But in this one thing Sukaracharya surpassed him.

So the gods said to Brihaspati, "Your son Coch is very clever. Perhaps he can become Sukaracharya's student. If he is a good student, Sukaracharya will teach him the mantra."

The gods were very tricky. They didn't tell Coch the real reason they were sending him to Sukaracharya. They led him to believe they were sending him there to become a devoted student and to learn how to use weapons and other useful things. Coch was an innocent young man and had no idea of what the gods were planning.

In those days even if someone was your enemy, if you went to him as a student that person would teach you, so Coch went to Sukaracharya and asked to become his student. Sukaracharya had a big heart and graciously accepted Coch as his student.

In time, Coch became Sukaracharya's favorite student.

The other disciples became jealous because their Master was paying so much attention to their enemy's son. They also saw that Sukaracharya's daughter, Debajani, was very fond of Coch. The two were the same age and Sukaracharya's disciples believed she hoped to marry Coch when they grew up.

Sukaracharya knew about his daughter's love for Coch and he had no objection to their marriage. He said, "With all my heart I love my daughter and I also love this boy." He was waiting for the day when they would be old enough to marry.

One of Coch's primary jobs was to take the cattle out to graze each morning. One morning while Coch was with the cattle, the other disciples killed him. When the young boy did not come back in the evening, Debajani became worried and went looking for him. She found him lying in the field and ran back home crying to her father. Sukaracharya went to where the boy was lying and uttered his special mantra in silence. The boy was instantly revived.

Sukaracharya and his daughter were happy, but the jealous disciples were miserable and angry, and decided the next day they would kill him again. This time, while he was in the field, they grabbed him and set fire to him so that he was burned to ashes. Then they made a special drink and put his ashes into it. They brought the drink to Sukaracharya and said, "We have made a very special drink for you. Will you taste it?"

Sukaracharya said, "Yes. I will taste it." As he drank, he felt uneasy. Then his daughter came running up and cried, "What have you done? I have just heard that your disciples burned Coch to ashes and then put his ashes into a special drink. Now you have drunk it and he is totally gone! You will not be able to revive him."

Sukaracharya said, "It is true. If I revive him, he will have to come out of me; then I will die. You must accept the fact that he is dead; or if I revive him and bring him out of my body, then you will lose me. What shall we do?"

The daughter began crying uncontrollably. Sukaracharya said, "All right, I am an old man. I have enjoyed life and have done many things, good and bad. What is the use of staying on earth any longer? It is time for me to retire. All of you leave me here. Secretly I will chant my special mantra. Then, since a portion of Coch still exists inside my body, I am sure he will be revived and come out of me, and I will die."

Sukaracharya chanted the mantra in silence and immediately Coch was revived. As soon as Coch came out of his Master's body, Sukaracharya died.

It happened that when he had been inside Sukaracharya, Coch had heard him chant the mantra inwardly–although Sukaracharya never chanted it out loud. In this way Coch learned the secret mantra. As soon as Coch was revived, out of his sincere gratitude he immediately touched his Master's feet and said, "Master, you have saved me." Then he used the same mantra to revive his Master. Sukaracharya immediately blessed Coch and said to him, "You have learned the mantra from me, and now you have saved me with it."

Coch said, "I did not learn it the first time you revived me. Only when you used the mantra in silence, and I was inside you, did I learn it."

Both Sukaracharya and Coch were alive and they were very happy. Then a sadness dawned on Debajani. Because Coch had come out of her father, he was now her brother, and they could not get married. But at least she had her father back.

Everything started with love. If the daughter had not loved Coch, then these things would not have happened, for the disciples of Sukaracharya would not have been so jealous. Then Coch showed his magnanimity when he revived his father's enemy, Sukaracharya. But in his willingness to sacrifice his own life for Coch, Sukaracharya was the one who really showed his heart's nobility and generosity, like a real Master.

Here the actual winners were the cosmic gods. Now both Sukaracharya and Coch had the power to revive the dead. From that time on the demon-disciples of Sukaracharya could not defeat the gods because both parties knew how to revive their dead soldiers.

The cosmic gods justified sending Coch to learn the mantra by saying, "We did the right thing because we have balanced our two sides; they are equally strong. This is the only way we will stop fighting."

When Sukaracharya's disciples came to know that the cosmic gods also had the power to revive their dead soldiers, they didn't want to fight anymore. Since both were now equally strong, the fighting between the gods and the demons came to an end.

Inside I live
Soulfully and sleeplessly.
Outside I give
Generously and unconditionally.

The Three Hosts

One day a king and his minister went out for a walk incognito. The king said to the minister, "I want to give a reward to anyone who is hospitable to us during our walk."

The king and the minister went up to one man and said, "We are travelers. This is a fine town and we would like to spend the night here. Could we stay at your house as guests?"

The man insulted them, saying, "How do I know you're not criminals?"

Then the king and the minister went up and knocked on somebody else's door. When the man opened the door they asked, "Can we can spend the night here? We are travelers and it's getting dark."

The man said, "First tell me how many of you there are. Then I'll decide."

The king said, "You see that we are only two. We don't have much money, but if you allow us to stay with you, before we leave tomorrow morning we'll pay you what we can."

Then the king said, "It is still somewhat light out, and your country is very beautiful. We'll walk around and come back in an hour or so."

So the king and minister continued walking. They approached another house and knocked on the door. The king said, "We're travelers. It's getting dark. Could we spend the night at your house?"

The man said, "Certainly! Just tell me how many of you there are."

The king said, "You can see we are only two." The king told that person also that they would come back in a while. Then they went back to the palace.

The minister had taken down the address of each person to whom they had spoken, and the following day the king summoned all three to the palace. To the one who had insulted him the king said, "I don't need you in my kingdom. When travelers come from a different kingdom, we must offer them shelter. You could see we were respectable. It was obvious we weren't thieves." And the king threw the man out of his kingdom.

To the second man the king gave a large sum of money. To the third one, who immediately offered shelter and only afterwards asked how many were in their party, the king gave his crown.

He told the man, "In this kingdom we need the kind of people who offer everything without hesitation and only then seek to determine how much is necessary. When we approached you, you didn't ask how many were in our party. You just said, 'Come, come!' The other man first asked how many we had. If we had more people, he might not have agreed to shelter us. We need more people like you."

So the third man received the crown from the king and took it home as his most treasured possession.

Only two miracles are
worth seeing:
The miracle of loving
And
The miracle of forgiving.

Babar's Heart of Forgiveness

The Mogul Emperor Babar was kind, generous and powerful. Once while he was away from his kingdom, his step-grandmother incited one of his cousins to stand against him. This particular cousin made friends with the chief of the army and a few important figures in the capital. When Babar tried to return to his kingdom, his whole army fought against him. They wouldn't allow him to come back. But Babar had quite a few followers outside his kingdom, and they helped him fight against his own people. Babar was so great and powerful that eventually he won the battle.

After he had won, Babar went and knelt down before his step-grandmother. He said to her with folded hands, "I don't hold anything against you. If a mother likes one son more than another son, what can the less favored son do? The mother should love all her children equally, but if she does not, the ones that are not in favor must not feel sorry for themselves. They should bear the same love for their mother as the ones who have her favor. So I don't hold anything against you. You have done the right thing, according to your light. Now let me have peace of mind." Then he placed his head on her lap and fell asleep.

A few hours later Babar woke up, only to see the main culprit, his cousin, standing in front of him. He had been arrested and brought to Babar by the Emperor's loyal followers. Babar stood up and embraced his cousin. Then he said, "You are at perfect liberty either to stay with me for the rest of your life or to leave my kingdom. If you leave my kingdom and want to live elsewhere, I will cover your expenses. If you want to continue here, you are free to do so. I feel no ill will toward you at all."

His cousin said to him, "Babar, I want to stay. If I leave, people will try to kill me. Not your favorites, but those who helped me fight against you will try to kill me in order to make you feel that they are your friends. So I want to stay here. I know you will never kill me. More than that, I know your forgiveness and compassion will be my eternal friends, and that you will eventually give me a high post."

Babar then gave him a broad smile of forgiveness and assurance.

*My heart's love-boat
Has room even for those
Who are suffering
From jealousy-monster.*

Babar Takes a Life

There was nothing that the great Emperor Babar would not do for his subjects. He regarded them as his children. From time to time Babar left his palace to walk along the streets of the city. He mixed with his subjects and saw how they lived. If he saw someone who was poverty stricken, he helped him out. People did not recognize him because he dressed simply on these ventures, and he wore a kind of turban over his crown so it was impossible for people to know what it was.

Now it happened that there was a young man who was very jealous of Babar because everyone admired and adored him. They extolled Babar to the skies for his bravery, kindness, nobility and other divine qualities. For this reason the young man had long harbored a desire to kill Babar. He had heard that sometimes the emperor walked unprotected in the city. He always carried a sword, hoping that someday he would meet the emperor when he was by himself and have the opportunity to kill him.

Usually when Babar went out, his guards secretly followed him to protect him. Babar didn't want anyone to go with him, but his guards were afraid for his safety.

On one particular afternoon the emperor managed to go out alone, without his guards. As Babar was walking along incognito, he saw a mad elephant charging down the street. People were shouting and running away from the elephant, and everybody was panicking. But there was one little, helpless child who could not run fast enough to get out of the way. Everybody was frightened to death, but nobody dared try to save the child. Just as the elephant was about to trample the little child, the emperor ran and snatched the child out of the way. Babar saved the child, but as he tumbled out of the way, his turban fell to the ground.

When the mad elephant had passed by, some men ran to pick up the turban of the brave hero. When they looked inside, they realized it was their emperor's crown. The young man who wanted to kill Babar was one of those who had seen the emperor save the life of the child. Although he himself had known that the child's life was in danger, he had not been brave enough to try to save him and had run away like everyone else. When he realized what had happened, he fell at Babar's feet and said, "Forgive me."

Babar said, "What have you done?"

The man said, "I have wanted to kill you for many years because I was jealous of the admiration you receive. Now I see you truly deserve it. As emperor, you are more precious to the kingdom than any of us, but you were ready to give up your own life to save a little child. What I have learned from you is that it is infinitely better to give life than to take life. Now, instead of taking your life, I am giving you mine. Please take my life." Then he offered Babar the sword with which he had planned to kill him.

Babar took the sword and said, "I taught you how to give life. Now I am going to take your life. Come with me. From now on you will be one of my bodyguards. I can see that you are sincere, and I am sure you will be a faithful guard."

So Babar took the man's life, only to make it into a useful and fruitful one. Instead of killing him, or instead of punishing him, Babar made the man one of his personal bodyguards.

It is an exceptional privilege
To have the beauty of
a serene mind,
The purity of a loving heart
And
The divinity of a humble life.

Nasir Uddin and the Pundit

ℜasir Uddin was a very pious king. He refused to take money from his kingdom's treasury for his own personal needs. To make extra money, he copied the Koran in his own handwriting and then sold the books. He also made a few other things to sell, and in this way he would cover his personal expenses.

One day a great pundit came to his palace to visit him. Nasir Uddin happened to be copying the Koran, and the pundit watched him for some time. At one point the king stopped writing and started talking to his guest. The pundit said to him, "Your Majesty, unfortunately you have made a mistake in a word you were copying."

Nasir Uddin circled the word that the pundit wanted to correct. Then he erased it and wrote in the word that the pundit suggested. The pundit was pleased that the king had listened to him. When he left the palace, however, the king erased the word and replaced it with the word that he had written originally.

His guards asked him, "Why are you doing that? If it was the right word in the first place, why did you change it?"

The king answered, "Although I may be king, he is a pundit, and he knows much more than I do in this field. Unfortunately, he happened to be mistaken in this case. But had I told him he was wrong, his pride would have been hurt. I wrote down the incorrect word so that he would not be embarrassed. But I don't want to leave the wrong word here. If I did, whoever buys this book would have the wrong version.

"There is no point in hurting people even if you are right. It is nothing for me to make myself humble, especially when it is a matter of book learning. Had he advised me about ruling my kingdom, do you think I would have listened to him? Managing my kingdom is a different story. But it is always good to show respect for someone's knowledge in their own field."

*Y our vision-light will have
No reality-delight
Unless your life becomes
The constant flow
Of a self-giving river.*

The Cow and the Pig

There was once a man who was very rich and very miserly at the same time. The villagers disliked him intensely. One day he said to them, "Either you're jealous of me or you don't understand my love of money–God alone knows. But you dislike me; that much I know. When I die, I won't take anything with me. I will leave it all for others. I will make a will, and I will give everything to charity. Then everyone will be happy."

Even then people mocked and laughed at him. The rich man said to them, "What is the matter with you? Can't you wait a few years to see my money go to charity?"

The villagers didn't believe him. He said, "Do you think I'm immortal? I'll die like everyone else, and then my money will go to charities." He couldn't understand why they didn't believe him.

One day he went for a walk. All of a sudden it started raining heavily, so he took shelter under a tree. Under this tree he saw a pig and a cow. The pig and the cow entered into conversation, and the man overheard what they were saying.

The pig said to the cow, "How is it that everybody appreciates you and nobody appreciates me? When I die, I provide people with bacon, ham and sausage. People can also use my bristles. I give three or four things, whereas you give only one thing: milk. Why do people appreciate you all the time and not me?"

The cow said to the pig, "Look, I give them milk while

I'm alive. They see that I am generous with what I have. But you don't give them anything while you're alive. Only after you're dead do you give ham, bacon and so forth. People don't believe in the future; they believe in the present. If you give while you are alive, people will appreciate you. It is quite simple."

From that moment on, the rich man gave all he had to the poor.

Now is the time
To make good use of time.
Today is the day
To begin a perfect day.

The Astrologer Fulfills His Prophecies

When a young man's parents died they left him a great deal of money. He was quite rich and didn't have to work. Instead of working, he enjoyed hobbies. One day he was interested in music. The next day he wanted to be a great tennis player. The next day it was something else. Because he couldn't stick to anything he accomplished nothing at all. He wallowed in the pleasures of wealth and wasted money. But he didn't worry because he still had plenty of money.

He started casting horoscopes and telling people what would happen in the future. Nobody took him seriously because astrology was only another hobby for him, but everybody liked to hear what he had to say. As long as he didn't create any problems, nobody minded.

One day his uncle came to visit him looking very sad. The young man asked his uncle, "Why are you so sad?"

His uncle said, "I am sad because I don't have any money. I am in tremendous financial difficulty."

The young man said, "Let me take a look at your horoscope. Let's see what the future holds."

When the astrologer looked at his uncle's horoscope he said, "I see that in a month's time, by a stroke of luck, you will get all the money you need."

The uncle asked, "Are you sure?"

The young man said, "Your horoscope clearly indicates that you will. I can see it. I'm certain your financial difficulties will end in a month's time."

The uncle was very happy to hear that he would get some money. He waited day after day, but nothing happened.

On the last day of the month the uncle happened to be passing by his nephew's house. The young man was in front of his house and the uncle said to him, "A month has passed and I haven't gotten any money. Why do you fool people like this? For God's sake, give up this astrology business. You were not meant to be an astrologer."

The young man said, "Uncle, I told you to wait for one month. The month is not yet over."

The uncle said, "You are so stupid! Today is the last day. Who is going to give me money? No one! Either you are a fool or a liar. You know nothing about astrology!"

The young man said, "Yes I do. And I know that you'll get the money. The day isn't over yet."

Then the so-called astrologer went into another room and came back with a large amount of money. He handed it to his uncle and said, "Look, my prophecy is true."

The uncle said, "Yes! Your prophecy has come true. I am so grateful to you."

At that moment a schoolteacher happened to be passing by. The schoolteacher didn't see the nephew giving money to his uncle. He only overhead the uncle praising his astrologer-nephew because the prophecy had come true.

Now for some time the teacher had been thinking of going to this astrologer to have his daughter's horoscope cast. So the teacher approached the young man and said, "I've got a problem. It is now time for my daughter's marriage. Can you tell me if there's a chance for her to find a good husband? I'd like her to marry a rich, well-educated man so that she won't have to worry about her future."

The young man looked at the daughter's horoscope and said, "In two months' time you will find the perfect husband for your daughter. From her horoscope I can see that she is a good girl. You will find the right person to marry her."

The teacher was excited and began preparing for his daughter's wedding. He even hired a special cook and servants for the ceremony. Meanwhile, the days were passing, and still he hadn't found a suitable husband for his daughter. But he had such faith in the young astrologer that he believed something would happen.

Finally, when the two months were almost up, the man went back to the astrologer and said, "Are you sure that my daughter will be married? I have made all the preparations. I've arranged for a priest and hired extra servants. I've bought jewelry for her wedding. But I haven't found a bridegroom. What will happen if your prophecy does not come true?"

The astrologer said, "Why do you have to worry? In this village is there anybody who is richer than I am? And do you not think I am handsome? Do you not think I am well-educated?"

The teacher said, "You? How can I expect you to marry my daughter?"

The astrologer said, "Why not?"

The teacher said, "Since you are rich, handsome and kindhearted, will you marry my daughter?"

The young man said, "Of course, of course! You don't have to worry. We'll be married tomorrow."

So the astrologer married the teacher's daughter, and in this way he kept his promise and made his prophecy come true.

His new wife was very smart. She had heard how her husband had given money to his uncle because his prophecy wasn't coming true. And she knew that he had to marry her in order to make his next prophecy come true. So she said, "I won't allow you to continue with this occupation. Since you have so much money, you don't have to work. But you do have to give up casting horoscopes because you don't know anything about astrology. If you really love me, then you have to give it up.

"You are the richest person in the village, the zamindar. You have so many servants. If occasionally you go to the fields to supervise, then our servants will do a better job and we will have a bumper crop. This can be your job."

So every day the young man would spend a few hours looking after the fields. The workers were very happy that he was showing such an interest in their work. The young man was happy knowing that he was accomplishing something positive each day. He had a reason to rise out of bed each morning.

About three months later his uncle came again to him and said, "Nephew, again I am in need of money. Can you cast my horoscope and see if there is any hope for me to get some money?" The uncle was hoping that his nephew would again give him money to fulfill his own prophecy.

The young man said, "I'm sorry. I've given up casting horoscopes. My wife said I was no good at it, so I gave it up."

*The promise-maker
Has a great mind.
The promise-fulfiller
Is a good heart.*

A Sincere Man's Promise

This is a true story about two friends. One day a young man said to his good friend, "I can see that some day you will become great and rich."

His friend scoffed, "Ridiculous! How will I become a great and rich man?"

The first friend said, "Yes, I can see it. It is written on your forehead."

The second one said, "All right, if I become great and rich, I will give you ten thousand rupees."

"Do you really mean it?" the first friend asked. "If so, then write it down."

The second one wrote down, "I will give you 10,000 rupees if ever I become rich and great," and he signed his name.

The young man kept the note that his friend had written, but he never took his friend seriously. The agreement was made as a joke. Now, it happened that in 10 or 12 years the one friend really did become rich and great, while the other unfortunately remained quite poor. By that time both friends had drifted apart and were leading their own lives. Even so, the poor friend continued to preserve the note, although he felt that since it was a joke, he would never receive the money.

Quite unexpectedly, the poor man fell seriously ill. Just before he died, he called his son, who was only seven years old, and said to him, "My son, please bring me the box that is near the window. Inside it there is something very precious that I have kept for you."

The son was so sad that his father was dying that he did not want to bring the box. He felt that nothing could be more precious than his father's life. But the father insisted, so the son went and got the box. Then the father said, "When I die . . ." and immediately the little boy and his mother started crying. But the father continued, "After I die, you go to this man and show him what he has written." The wife and son looked at the paper and were surprised to learn that the rich man had promised to give his friend ten thousand rupees. But at that moment they could think of nothing but their beloved who was about to leave them.

Soon the man died. Their friendship had faded so much that the rich man, who was once the poor man's best friend, did not even come to see him before he left this world. But after three or four weeks' time the son took the note to the rich man. The rich man had many servants. At first they didn't want to allow this little boy to bother their master. But finally, when they saw he was only an innocent child, they allowed him to come in.

The boy gave the rich man the note. The rich man read it and asked, "Did I write this?"

The boy said, "I do not know. Before he died, my father gave it to me to give to you." The son was near tears. The rich man summoned one of his secretaries and explained, "I promised this boy's father many years ago that I would give him 10,000 rupees if I became rich and great. I have been rich for seven years; please calculate how much interest I have to give him in addition to the 10,000 rupees."

The secretary told him, "An additional 7,000 rupees, which makes it 17,000 altogether."

The rich man immediately issued a check for 17,000 rupees and gave it to the little boy, saying, "Take this directly to your mother. Don't go anywhere else first."

This is how one sincere man kept his promise.

*From now on I shall keep
The suspicion-snake behind me,
The faithfulness-dog beside me,
The promise-deer before me.*

The Zamindar's Servant

Ⱥ village zamindar (a landowner and village tax collector) and his wife had a number of goats. A servant, a young boy, looked after them. The zamindar liked the boy very much, but his wife was suspicious of him. Fortunately the lad did not know this. The wife was very clever. Outwardly she was kind, polite and affectionate to him, but inwardly she was hostile and mistrustful.

One day a friend came to the zamindar's home and saw that he was very sad. The friend asked, "Why are you sad?"

The zamindar answered, "My wife and I are not getting along because of this servant. We each have a different opinion of him."

The friend said, "Don't worry. I can solve the problem and tell you whether he is good or bad."

One day while the servant was watching the goats in a field, the master's friend came up to him and said, "This particular goat is so beautiful. Will you sell it to me for five rupees?"

The boy answered, "No, I am sorry. I cannot sell it."

The friend asked again, "Will you sell it to me for 10 rupees?"

The boy said, "No, I am sorry."

"Twenty rupees?" the friend asked.

The servant said, "If you want to buy the goat, go to my master and give him the 20 rupees. If my master says he will sell it, then I will give it to you."

The friend said, "Who wants to go to your master? His

house is quite far. Let me give you 30 rupees. I am sure that your master does not give you enough salary. Keep the 30 rupees and tell your master that the goat was stolen. Your master has so many goats. He won't even know it is gone."

"Oh no," the boy said, "I can't do that. He would know. And even if he didn't notice, I know how many goats he has, so I would know that one was missing."

The friend said, "Just take 30 rupees and give me the goat. Then go and give your master the money and tell him you have sold it."

The boy said, "No, I am sorry. I can't sell it without my master's permission."

"If I give you 100 rupees, will you give me the goat?" the friend said. "Then you can keep all the money."

"I am not a thief," the servant said. "I could never keep the money."

The friend said, "You could give him 70 rupees and keep 30 for yourself. Or you could just tell him the goat was stolen and keep all the money for yourself."

"I could never do that," the young man said.

But the man persisted, and the servant finally conceded, "If you really want to give me 100 rupees for one goat, then I will accept the money and give it to my master."

The zamindar's friend was very curious to see what the servant would do with the money. He thought, "Either he will give his master a little less or tell him the goat was stolen. No matter what he does, I will be able to tell his master the true story."

The servant went to his master and gave him the hundred rupees. He said, "Master, forgive me. Without your permission I sold a goat for a hundred rupees. I knew that the goat was only worth five rupees, but this man insisted on giving me a hundred for it. I thought that you would be very happy to get 100 rupees for a goat that is worth only five. Now you can buy many more goats."

The wife said to the servant, "I wish to speak to my husband privately for a minute. Would you please go away from here now?"

Then the wife said to her husband, "I don't trust him. I tell you, he sold it at an even higher price and is giving us only part of it." She did not know that it was the zamindar's friend who had bought the goat.

Just then the zamindar's friend arrived at his house and asked, "What is happening?"

The zamindar said, "Our servant tells us he sold a goat for a hundred rupees. I don't suspect him of wrongdoing, but my wife, as usual, does. She feels that he has sold the goat for a still higher price and kept some money for himself."

The friend said, "You will never find anybody in your lifetime as honest and sincere as this servant. It was I who bought the goat for a hundred rupees. I tried to persuade him to keep the money for himself. I was testing him. But each and every time he proved his honesty. I have examined him thoroughly. He is sincerity incarnate."

The zamindar said to his wife, "I told you so!"

The wife said, "It is always good to test people in this way. From now on, I will trust this boy as my own son."

I have lost my patience-seed.
I have lost my flower-heart.
I have lost my satisfaction-soul.
All this is due
To my deplorably stupid jealousy.

The Thief's Gold Cup

There were two thieves who were good friends and, at the same time, were very jealous of each other. Such is human life: friendship and jealousy go together.

One night, after they had gone out stealing, they met in the street. One of them had a beautiful golden cup. The other thief said, "How did you get that?"

His friend said, "I stole it from a hermit's house."

The first thief said, "How could a hermit own such a beautiful gold cup?"

His friend said, "That I don't know, but the hermit has many disciples. Perhaps one of them gave him this. He doesn't care if he has a gold cup or an earthen pot. Most of the time he just sits at the foot of a tree near his small house and prays and meditates. He doesn't care about his possessions. His disciples put expensive things in his house, but he is above all that. He is not attached to material things."

The first thief was jealous that his friend had gotten such a beautiful gold cup. Finally he said, "Well, I have decided that I will give up stealing."

His friend said, "What! Why would you do that?"

The first thief answered, "Stealing is not a good thing. I have decided to return all the things that I have stolen to their rightful owners. True, some things I have already sold, and those I cannot give back. But whatever I have that I know belongs to certain individuals, I am going to return and confess that I have stolen it.

"Everybody looks down on me because they know I am a thief. Therefore, I have decided that I want to give up stealing. Then people will appreciate and love me. I want to be liked, so I will become a good person. I am going to start tomorrow."

The other thief was amazed and jealous that his friend had thought of this idea first. He said, "You are starting tomorrow?"

"Yes," said the first thief.

"Then I am starting right now," said his friend. He ran to the hermit's hut and went in. Bowing down, he said, "Please give me some advice. During the day I was very busy. That is why I am coming at night to ask for your advice. Actually, it is not my problem; it is someone else's problem. If you can solve my friend's problem, I will be very grateful."

"What is his problem?" asked the hermit.

The man said, "My friend is a thief and he claims he is going to return the things that he has stolen and lead a new and better life. What should he do now?"

"What do you mean?" asked the hermit.

"Suppose I have stolen something from someone. If I want to give it back, am I doing the right thing by telling him that I have stolen it and by making a confession?"

The hermit said, "You are doing the right thing if you make a confession and give back the things that you have taken. Then God will forgive you."

The thief said, "In case the owner does not want to take it back, what should the person do? The owner may be disgusted and think that the object is polluted because it was been stolen by a low-class thief. A thief is impure."

"In that case," said the hermit, "the thief can keep it. It is up to the owner whether he takes it back or not. If the owner does not take it back, then the thief cannot be blamed for keeping it."

The thief then took out the cup and gave it to the hermit. The hermit asked, "Where is it from?"

The thief said, "From your house."

The hermit was always in trance so he did not recognize it. He said, "You have taken it from my house?"

"Yes," said the thief. "Please take it back."

The hermit said, "Since you have it now, it is your possession. You need it more than I do. Otherwise, you would not have taken it. I pray to God and meditate on God. Why do I need expensive things? An earthen cup is more than enough for me. I am not suggesting that you are impure. You are also God's child. But I didn't know this cup was mine and I don't need it. It should be yours. I don't have any claim on it."

When the thief returned, his friend was still waiting for him. The friend was surprised to see that he still had the beautiful gold cup. The thief said, "I went to see the hermit, but he wouldn't take it back. He said he didn't need it and that I need it more than he does."

The other thief was even more jealous that his friend still had the beautiful gold cup. He had not really planned to turn over a new leaf by returning all of his stolen goods. It was out of jealousy that he had tried to trick his friend into returning the cup. His scheme did not work and what was worse, his jealousy had increased, for his friend had become an infinitely better person.

Selflessness means
That the breath of happiness
Is here
And the life of happiness
Is now.

The Notorious Son

A young boy was notorious for quarreling with people and insulting them. His father had died several years earlier, so his mother had to raise him by herself. She was very sad because he would not behave. She was at her wit's end. The villagers spoke ill not only of him, but also of his mother because they thought she was indulgent. Actually, it was just the opposite. His mother was very strict with him, but he wouldn't listen to her.

One day he insulted an elderly man and the villagers wanted to thrash him. The mother came and pleaded with the villagers. She said, "True, my son is wrong, but please forgive him and forgive me as well. I'm trying to help him."

The village head was kind enough to release the son because of the mother's pleas. The mother brought the boy home and said, "I will soon die because I am old. After my death, perhaps you will start heeding my advice and become a good boy. I will leave some money for you when I die, so use the money and think of me. Right now, because you are mischievous and naughty I am miserable. I am going to send you away to a boarding school."

When the boy went to the boarding school, he argued with his teachers and the other students. Then one day he got word that his mother had died. He returned to his village shedding bitter tears, and said, "Mother, I could not please you when you were alive. But I now take this oath: I will become an excellent boy." From then on he never quarreled. He became simple, honest and kindhearted.

Although his mother had left him some money, it was not enough for him to continue his studies for very long. Since he didn't have any real interest in school, after studying for a year or two he began looking for a job. Finally, the village zamindar gave him some work taking care of his garden and looking after his children.

One day the boy was holding the garden hose in one arm and the zamindar's youngest child in his other arm. The zamindar happened to pass by and said, "When you water the garden, put the child down. For everything there is a time. You cannot do both jobs at the same time and do them well. You can water the garden now and later show your affection to the child."

The boy obediently put the child on the ground and continued watering the garden. Ten minutes later the zamindar's wife came by and saw the child sitting on the ground while the boy watered the garden. She was furious. She said, "How dare you keep my child on the ground. Can't you hold him in one arm? With one arm you can water the garden and with the other you can carry my child. Besides, who wants you to water plants? Right now you should take care of my youngest child and forget about watering the garden."

The boy kept silent and stopped watering the garden to take care of the child. In this way he pleased both his master and his master's wife.

By now everyone in the village liked this young man because he was kindhearted and a good worker. Now, it happened that in the school where he used to study, a younger student had developed the same kind of mischievous nature that this boy used to possess. This younger student always fought with his teachers and the other students. His mother was in distress all the time because of her son's bad behavior.

This ill-behaved student was very jealous of the zamindar's servant. His mother said to him, "I know you are jealous of the zamindar's servant. But by being jealous you are not going to get his good qualities. Only by admiring him and doing what he does will you be able to develop the same qualities one day."

The son didn't listen to his mother. He continued to do mischievous things, arguing with people and hitting them. One day some stronger boys got angry with him and beat him up. He ran home crying.

He decided to go to the zamindar's servant to see how he could change his nature. He said to the servant, "You are kind, good and modest. You have no pride, anger or restlessness. How did you develop these good qualities?"

The servant told him, "My mother always begged me to be good, but I wouldn't listen. When she died, I took an oath to change my nature, to be good. When you try to please people they become grateful to you and proud of you."

The servant continued, "This morning I was watering the plants, holding the hose in one arm and my master's youngest child in the other arm. My master got mad and said I should not try to do two things at once. He said I should put the child on the ground while I watered the garden with both hands. So I put down the child with utmost humility and began watering the garden. The master was very pleased that I had listened to him.

"A few minutes later my master's wife saw me watering the garden. She insulted me and said, 'Why have you left the child on the ground? Is he inferior to the plants?' She wanted me to pick the child up immediately. She said I should stop watering the plants and take care of the child.

So I stopped watering the garden.

"I didn't lose anything by making both my master and his wife happy. I always try to please my master and his wife. Because of this they are fond of me. In your case, too, if you practice being peaceful and harmonious with your mother, your teachers and friends, they will be happy. Only by giving happiness to others can you become happy yourself.

"I feel awful that I waited until my mother died before I tried to please her. I advise you to change your nature now and please your mother while she is still alive. Then you will see how much joy you will find. The enjoyment you get now by being mischievous is false. It is stupid. If you bring joy to others you will be happy."

The young boy went and told his mother what the servant had said. His mother went to the zamindar's house and approached the servant. She told him, "I won't allow you to be anybody's servant. From now on I want you to be my oldest son. I will take care of you and you can continue your studies. Your mother is not on earth, so I want to be your mother and offer you the same kind of affection and love."

The woman brought the boy home and sent both her sons to school to complete their higher studies.

Every day you should try
To set a personal record
In your unconditional
self-giving.

The Pilgrimage

Once there were two neighbors who were friends and, at the same time, rivals. Both of them were very shrewd and miserly. At times they were absolutely, unthinkably undivine.

One day they decided to go on a pilgrimage. Their wives made up delicious baskets of food for them and they left very early in the morning.

After they had walked for two hours, it was breakfast time. One of them said, "Let us not stop for breakfast. We don't need to eat right now."

The other one said, "I agree. Let's keep walking and stop later for lunch instead."

So they continued walking. When lunch time came, one of them said, "I'm not hungry. If you want to eat, go ahead, but I'm not hungry in the least."

The other one said, "I'm not hungry either. Let's walk until we are tired. Then we can stop and eat."

Both of them were perfect rogues. Each one thought that his own wife had made the best food and didn't want to share it with the other. Each one thought, "If we walk for some time, then my friend will become tired and fall asleep. Then I'll be able to eat my food all by myself. I don't want to share any of it with him."

They walked until it was evening and they were both very tired. After they stopped, each one was waiting for the other to fall asleep. They waited and waited. Finally, both of them fell asleep.

The following morning when they woke up, they saw that their food was crawling with ants. Instead of blaming themselves, they got mad at their wives! "We didn't check the food when they gave it to us. Now we find ants all over it. When we go home, we'll give them a piece of our mind," they agreed.

But they were still tired and decided to rest a while longer. When they woke up a few hours later, they found rats eating what was left of their food. They were so disgusted that they immediately went home and insulted and scolded their wives.

Their wives said, "Why didn't you eat the food we gave you during the day?"

Each one told his wife, "I didn't want to share any of your excellent food with that rascal. It took him so long to fall asleep that I fell asleep too."

Each wife told her husband, "Since both of you are so greedy and miserly, when you start on your pilgrimage again, I will give you simple food–a loaf of bread–which you can share with your friend. He will be pleased if you share it. Since you are travelling together, you can at least have this much friendship."

One wife made bread that was very salty and the other made bread with no salt at all. Since their wives had told them that the food was very simple, both men were extremely generous. One of them said, "I am sure your wife is a good cook. Let's exchange food."

The other one said, "That is an excellent idea."

So they exchanged their food and started eating. The one who got the salty bread said, "Your wife can't cook!"

The other one responded with, "Your wife can't cook! There's no salt in this bread. It's tasteless."

The first man said, "My wife is an excellent cook."

The other one said, "Your wife! Then how is it that she forgot to put salt in the bread?"

The first one said, "How is it that your wife put too much salt in her bread?"

They continued to fight until their pilgrimage came to an end, and again they went home and insulted their wives.

Each of them said to his wife, "You made horrible food. I was ashamed."

Their wives said, "We thought that you were good friends. If you had shared your food with each other, there would have been no problem. One loaf of bread had too much salt and the other had no salt. If you had shared, it would have been delicious for both of you."

The husbands learned an important lesson from their wives: When you share with your friends, you will lead a more fulfilling life.

If you want to be a person
of integrity
Then what you need
Is a heart of morning purity
And a life of evening simplicity.

The Honesty Diploma

Shere was a very rich village zamindar who was also a great philanthropist. Everyone liked him. Once he decided that for three days he would give rice, vegetables and money to the poor–and only to the poor.

One poor man received a very heavy sack of rice. Because he was such a poor man this made him very happy. When he came home and emptied the sack into storage bins, he found 20 gold coins mixed in with the rice. His wife was delighted. But the husband said, "The zamindar didn't intend to give me gold. He gave me rice. This is a mistake. I should return the coins."

The wife said, "Don't be a fool! We're poor. Take the gold to the market and exchange it for money."

The husband said, "No, I can't." And so they fought until the husband reminded his greedy wife that it was he who had brought the rice and gold home in the first place.

The following day he went back to the rich man. "You were so kind to give us things we needed. I found these 20 gold coins in the rice sack. I've come to return them. Although I am a beggar, I know this was a mistake and I am an honest man."

The rich man was moved by the poor man's sincerity, He said, "No, keep them. And because of your sincerity, I'll give you double the amount. You brought me 20 gold coins; you'll leave with 40. I give these to you personally so you know there's no mistake."

A greedy businessman happened to overhear the story

and he came up with a brilliant idea. He went to the poor man and said, "I heard that you have some gold coins. Do you want to sell a few to me?"

The poor man said, "Certainly. How many would you like to buy?"

The businessman bought six coins from the poor man. Then he put on beggar's clothes and went to the rich man's house. "I will do the same thing the beggar did and I will double my wealth," he thought. "Since over the past three days hundreds and hundreds of beggars have received bags of food from the zamindar, I am sure that he will not remember that I was not one of them."

So the businessman went to the zamindar and said, "Yesterday you gave me three gold coins but magically they have become six gold coins today. I have come to give back the original ones, while I am keeping the other three."

The zamindar said, "You are the only person to whom I gave coins whose wealth has increased. One man brought back the same amount I gave him. But in your case the amount increased. I am happy for you. Now, what can I do for you?"

The businessman-beggar said, "If you are impressed with my honesty because I'm returning these three coins, you can give me more. Had I not returned these coins, you would not have known the original three produced three more. If you value honesty, then give me a few more coins."

The rich man said, "You really deserve much more. Since from three coins you have got six, let me do one thing. I will give you something much more important that a few more gold coins."

The businessman was excited and curious. He said, "Please tell me what it is."

The zamindar asked his servant to write out an "honesty diploma." The servant wrote it out and the zamindar put it on this fellow's back and signed it. Then he told the businessman-beggar, "With this diploma you can announce to the whole world that you are the most honest man. I have not given an 'honesty diploma' to anyone else. But you deserve it."

I gave God what I have
And what I am:
My willingness.
God is now giving me
What He has and what He is:
His Fullness.

The Heaviest Load

A spiritual Master went out for a picnic with a group of 20 disciples. The disciples were pleased to be going out with their Master. The Master told them, "I have 20 bags for you to carry. They contain things we'll use today. Please select a bag to carry." Then he added, "But mind you, you can't trade the bag once you take it."

The disciples started lifting up all the bags to find the lightest ones, except one fellow who was looking for the heaviest one. The other disciples thought he was a real fool. They were amused that this fool would carry the heaviest load, while theirs were comparatively light.

After they had walked for four or five hours the Master said, "Let us sit down and eat. Please empty the bag that has the food in it. We'll carry the other bags to our next destination. There we'll see beautiful trees and flowers. Then we'll go home."

The disciples sat down to eat. When they opened their bags, they discovered that the heavy one had all the food in it. The other ones contained sand, clay, broken pots and other worthless things. The disciple with the heaviest bag emptied it at the request of the Master and everyone ate. When they set out for their second destination, the disciple who had the heaviest load was now carrying an empty bag.

When they reached the second destination, an orchard, they picked fruits and admired the beautiful scenery. Afterward, they walked to a museum. Finally, they had a six-hour walk back home.

When they had returned home, the Master said, "I told you that you couldn't change your bags. The one who had the heaviest load in the beginning later had the lightest. As for the rest of you, your bags were lighter to begin with, but you had to carry them much farther. The one who chose the heaviest bag was good and kindhearted. The rest of you rogues had to carry rubbish for the entire trip!"

The Master said to his rogue-disciples, "You are my third-class disciples and he is my first-class disciple. The one who wants to carry everybody's load is the one who is really a first-class disciple!"

𝒟o not allow
your pure flower-heart
To inherit the shameless
corruption
Of your blind and wild mind.

The Brass Pot

There was a village diver to whom everybody turned whenever something valuable fell into the pond. He was the one who would find the object for them, and the villagers paid him for his work. This is how he earned his living.

One day the wife of the village head saw the diver carrying a very beautiful brass pot. Someone had given him this pot as payment for his finding something in the pond. As soon as she saw it, the wife of the village leader became very excited and said, "Will you lend me that beautiful pot? I am having guests tonight for a special dinner, and I want them to think that I have an expensive pot. I'll only keep it for two or three days, and then I'll return it to you." Because her husband was so powerful, the diver had to give it to her if he wanted to stay out of trouble.

Two or three days passed and the woman had not returned the pot. The diver was afraid and embarrassed to ask her for it. He said, "Something has to be done, but what can I do? I'm helpless."

Finally, the woman sent a vessel back to the diver. It was not a brass pot but an earthen pot, with a note inside. The note said, "One of my servants washed the pot and as soon as water touched it, it became earthen. I'm sorry that I'm unable to return the pot the way I got it."

When the diver got the note, he was angry. He said, "O God, she tricked me! But how can I fight with the wife of the head of the village?"

Two years passed. One day, the village head's wife was showing off her beautiful brass pot to her friends. She had just had another dinner and she was bragging to her friends while washing the pot in the pond, when all of a sudden the vessel dropped into the water.

Now it was necessary for someone to dive into the water and find the pot. The village head was very clever. He told his wife, "If we call the village diver and he finds it, he'll know we lied." So they called in another diver to look for the brass vessel. The diver spent hours and hours, but he was not as expert as the village diver and he could not find it.

The wife was feeling cocky. She said to her husband, "By this time I'm sure that the village diver has forgotten that I took his pot. Anyway, he won't be able to prove it's the same one, and if our guards are watching him when he dives, how can he take it back?"

So the village head called the diver and said, "Will you help us? We dropped a beautiful brass pot into the pond."

The diver, who was certain it was the pot they had taken from him, said, "I can help. There's one small problem. I am running a very high fever today. If you insist, I can do it today, but I am quite sick and would prefer to dive tomorrow."

The village head said, "It has already been in the pond for a week. We can wait another night."

When the diver left, the wife of the village head began to tremble. She said, "What will happen if he tells people that we took this pot?" But after thinking for a moment, she continued, "We are rich and powerful. We can silence him if he argues with us."

That night the diver secretly dove into the pond and found the lost brass vessel. Then he replaced it with the earthen pot that the wife of the village head had given him two years before.

The following day the diver came to the village head and said, "Do you still want me to try to find the pot?"

"Yes," he answered.

The diver said, "I can't promise you that I'll be able to find it. In this world, no one is perfect. If it's God's Will, I'll find it."

The village leader said, "It is not God's Will; it's my will that you find it. That's enough!"

"Certainly," said the diver. "You're my lord, so there is no difference between your will and God's Will."

The village head was so flattered! He and his wife and children all went to the pond to watch the diver look for the pot. In 10 or 15 minutes the diver brought up the earthen pot.

The wife cried, "How can the pot be earthen? It was brass. How could this happen?"

The diver said, "I am sorry. This is what I found. You can ask somebody else to look if you like. Anyway, two years ago, when you were washing a brass pot you had borrowed from me, it turned to earth. If one brass pot turned to earth just from being washed, it's reasonable to expect another to change after being in water for a week. If you think your brass vessel is still in the pond, then send someone else to find it!"

The village head and his wife got the point. That night, the village head went to the diver's house and said, "What can I do? My wife is so fond of that brass vessel. I know she lied to you about the pot two years ago, and I had to stand up for her. Now, for God's sake, I want to keep my prestige. Take money from me, as much as you want. But just give me back the brass pot. I know it is yours, but let me buy it from you."

The village head bought the pot and took it home. The following day he asked his friends and neighbors to come to his house to see the pot. He was such a rogue! He told them, "I gave the diver a huge amount of money to go look in the pond once more. You people were not there, but he went there and found the one that we had lost."

The village head showed the pot to his wife and their friends and they all agreed that it was the same brass pot. "You see," said the village head, "money talks!"

The village head made everybody think that the diver was a rogue, but the village head was the real rogue!

How can you lose
In the battlefield of life
If you are already
well-acquainted
With the real in you:
Your heart's aspiration-cry?

The King and the Sword

𝒜 great Indian king once went on a boat trip on the
Ganges. He and his attendants saw a man swimming
behind them. It was the spiritual master Troilanga Swami.
It happened, in an hour or so, that Troilanga Swami swam
near the boat smiling, so they helped him into the boat.
All the people there knew him and had tremendous
respect, love and veneration for him. The king was also
pleased to see him because he too admired him.

The king had a sword hanging around his waist.
Troilanga Swami took it from him and examined it and
played with it like a child. Then suddenly he threw it into
the Ganges. The king was furious. He had received this
sword for his valor and merit; he was angry that he had
lost such a precious thing. He wanted to punish Troilanga
Swami but everybody protested: "Oh no, he is a saint; you
can't do that. It will be a terrible thing if you touch him."

The king said, "If you people are not willing to punish
him, then once we land I will get other people who will
gladly listen to me and punish this man."

When they were about to reach the shore, Troilanga
Swami, who was seated in the boat, placed his hand in the
water. All of a sudden two shining swords appeared in his
hand. They were identical, and both looked exactly like
the one he had thrown into the Ganges. Everybody was
astonished. The Master said to the king, "O king, now find
the one that belongs to you."

The king didn't know which one was actually his. Then

Troilanga Swami said to him, "You fool, you don't know which one belongs to you? You don't know your own possession?" Then he threw away the one that was not the king's and said, "In this world nothing remains with you. When you die, everything you have will remain here. To the Real in you I say, 'Don't live in the world of enjoyment. Remain in the world of aspiration. Remain in the world of Light, Peace and Bliss. You are a king, but you are a fool as well. Be wise. Only then will you have true happiness in life. Be spiritually wise!' "

Commentary:

Unless and until we become spiritually wise, we shall never know what our true possession is. Our true possession, our eternal possession, our only possession, is our love of God. There cannot be anything else here on earth or there in Heaven for us to claim as our own. Only our love of God–our constant, soulful and self-giving love of God–can be our eternal possession. This possession will always remain safe, and we ourselves will also be safe only when we claim this possession as our own.

Once we know that we have love of God in abundant, boundless and infinite measure, then God's possession, which is His entire creation, immediately becomes our possession as well. Our love of God claims God, and the moment we offer our love to God, God's creation immediately becomes ours as well. His entire creation comes from His Vision, and He and His Vision are inseparable. When we claim God with our love, God's Concern and God's creation immediately claim us; for the sole possessor is God and no one else.

Here on earth everything that we can see, we try to claim. Everything that is around us also wants to claim us. But we cannot claim others and they cannot claim us, for we see that something is missing in them and they see that the same thing is missing in us. What is missing is love of God. This is the seed, the possibility, which eventually grows into the inevitable, the fruit.

Your heart must become
A sea of love.
Your mind must become
A river of detachment.

The World-Renunciation Song

One day Troilanga Swami was with his disciples when a nicely dressed, middle-aged Bengali gentleman wearing a new garment and perfumed with oil came to him. To the disciples' wide surprise, Troilanga Swami embraced the gentleman.

Everybody said, "How can you embrace someone who is so sophisticated and worldly? He is not spiritual."

Troilanga Swami said to them, "You fools, you don't recognize him. You would have to give up everything in life, renounce everything, in order to come to his spiritual state of consciousness. In your highest state of consciousness you cannot equal him. For him to wear clean, ironed clothes or to use perfume is nothing. He has reached such a spiritual height that he will not be affected no matter what he wears or what he does. You can't judge people by their outer appearance. He is a great seeker, an extraordinary soul."

Troilanga Swami's words proved true. The man's name was Shyama Charan Lahiri and he was later known as a great spiritual Master.

Commentary:

If one knows how to sing the world-renunciation-song well, then one can never be tempted by the world-possession-song, not to speak of the world-temptation-dance. His divine realization is not affected in the inner world, his human performance is not affected in the outer world. He is like a boat that is in the water and, at the same time, is not affected by the water.

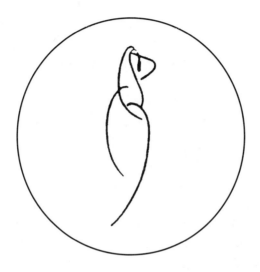

If you give God your heart's
Dearest treasure, surrender,
Then God will grant you
His Vision's
Dearest treasure, peace.

The Diamond Ring

A certain king was a devotee of Bhaskarananda and he visited his Master quite often. One day Bhaskarananda took him to a pond and casually asked the king to give him his diamond ring. Bhaskarananda looked at it closely. Then he threw it into the pond.

The king was not disturbed at all. He thought, "Perhaps I was too attached to it; therefore, the Master has thrown it in the water. Or perhaps the Master is just playing a game and will bring it back to me. I'm sure he has that kind of spiritual power. Anyway, whatever his reason, he's done it for my own good."

Bhaskarananda and the king had a long conversation about spirituality, and the Master told many spiritual secrets to the king. Then the Master said, "Don't you want to have your ring back?"

The king said, "It's up to you. If you want to, you can give it back. Otherwise, you can leave it at the bottom of the pond."

Bhaskarananda said, "All right, I want to give it back to you. Just touch the water with your hand."

The Master had thrown the ring from the spot where they were standing, but the king decided to go to the other side of the pond in order to see if the ring would reappear on that side. As he touched the water with his hand, 16 rings of the same type appeared. He could not tell which one was his.

"Since you are not attached to your ring," said Bhaskar-

ananda, "I am giving it back." Then the Master threw 15
of the rings back into the pond and gave the king the one
that was his.

Commentary:

*Possession is not happiness. Surrender and oneness with
the Master bring true happiness. With our human will we
possess, create and build the world of our imaginary liking. With our divine will we develop the capacity to have a
free access to God's ever-transcending Vision and ever-
manifesting Reality. The Master is at once the embodiment
of God's Vision-Height and His Reality-Depth.*

When I am matter-bound,
My world within is chaotic
And
My world without is chaotic.

When I am Spirit-free,
My world within
Is harmony-song
And
My world without
Is harmony-dance.

The Hindu-Muslim Compromise

Devadas, a well-known Hindu scholar, went to live and meditate in a Muslim area. In the middle of the night he blew a conch shell and rang a bell. Muslims are dead-set against using conchs and bells, and they warned the Hindu sadhu that they would punish him severely if he didn't stop doing this. The following night he blew the conch and rang the bell louder than ever. Muslim soldiers came to arrest him, but when they entered his room, to their wide surprise they saw his head had been severed from his body and was lying on a chair, and his limbs were all scattered around the room. But there was no blood. The soldiers didn't want to touch the body, so they left.

In a few minutes' time they heard the bell and the sound of the conch, so they rushed back, only to find the same scene again. Trembling and afraid, they left again, only to hear the conch and the bell a few minutes later. This time they were furious. When they returned to the room, Devadas was there in his normal human form.

"What can you do to me?" he said. "You have just seen twice what I can do. Before you arrest me, I will disassemble myself."

When the soldiers reported the matter to the Muslim chief, the chief said to them, "It is not a good idea to fight with a man who has such extraordinary spiritual power. The best thing is to surrender to him and ask if he would like to have a temple built. I shall pay for it. Let him peacefully pray and meditate there."

Devadas was extremely pleased with the Muslim chief's offer. The Muslim chief erected a beautiful temple for him, and Devadas, in deep gratitude, stopped blowing the conch and ringing the bell.

Commentary:

The Hindu and the Muslim are like two powerful branches of the reality-tree, which is all oneness-freedom. But the day-to-day life of human beings is so complicated that no matter what people do, we get irritated or feel insecure.

The Master showed that he had the body-reality to manifest the Supreme and the soul-reality to realize the Supreme. He disassembled and assembled his body in order to show others that medical science does not have the last word on God's creation, or man's life and death. It is only the inscrutable Will of the Supreme that operates in and through the spiritual Master.

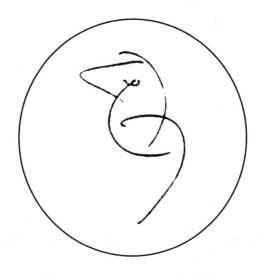

Life
Can be stronger
Than death
If man learns
Carefully and unmistakably
The language of love.

Divine Love Consoles Human Loss

A middle-aged disciple of Swami Nigamananda died of an incurable disease. His mother and his wife were thrown into a sea of sorrow. The mother was practically insane with grief. She said to a picture of their Master that was hanging on the wall, "Why do we keep you? You have no power; you're useless! I'm going to throw you in the pond!"

She grabbed the picture and headed toward the pond. All of a sudden she heard someone behind her crying, "Mother! Mother!" with a sorrowful voice. She turned and saw their Guru, Nigamananda, with tearful eyes saying to her, "Mother, let us go back home. Don't cry for your son anymore. I will be your son. He is with me, inside me."

The woman was greatly consoled and returned to her house with the picture of her Guru. At the hour all this occurred Nigamananda was actually 400 miles away, giving spiritual lessons to disciples living at his ashram.

Commentary:

Unlike divine love and divine worship, human love and human adoration are always based on personal interest. Whenever personal interest is in the picture, the closeness of inner oneness can never be achieved. At that time the seeker finds himself divided even from his dear ones by inner walls. Attachment to the world leads eventually to destruction.

You can forget everything
If you want to.
But don't forget one thing:
You are God's child,
God's very, very own.

Bama Eats the Temple Food

Bama Kshepa, a very poor young boy, used to frequent a temple that was owned by a queen and dedicated to the goddess Tara. One day he went into the temple and ate all the sanctified food that had been offered to the goddess. When the head priest and the guard saw what Bama had done, they struck him mercilessly.

That night the queen had a frightening dream. She saw the goddess Tara weeping in front of her. Although she was delighted to see the goddess, she was sad to see her weeping.

Then goddess Tara showed the queen her back, which was bleeding. "My dearest son, Bama, ate the food that was left for me in the temple. Your priest and your guard have beaten him mercilessly. If a son can't eat his mother's food, who can?"

The queen did not know who Bama was, but the next morning she asked the priest and the guard to bring him to her. They looked for him, but he was nowhere to be found. It took them three days to find Bama. He was still suffering from the pain of the beating, so they were very kind, affectionate and apologetic to him. When they brought him to the queen, she looked at him and felt miserable.

The queen said to Bama, "From now on this temple is yours. Before we place food in it, we'll feed you first. This is what the goddess Tara wants from me. I'll feed you before I offer her food in the temple." Bama was delighted. From that day on, his poverty was a thing of the past.

Since during the day
He sings soulful God-songs,
At night God allows him
To have beautiful
God-dreams.

The Wonderful Singer

There was a singer who put everybody to sleep when he sang. As soon as he began to sing, his audience would fall asleep. They would wake up hours later when the power of his singing had worn off.

Some said that he was such an excellent singer that he put everyone's soul to sleep. Others said that he was such a horrible singer that people slept rather than listen to him. So there were two schools of thought about the singer. One deeply appreciated his musical talent; the other did not appreciate him at all. But they all went to hear him sing.

One day, two burglars came to the singer and said, "You are such a great singer. We want to hire you. If we give you a lot of money, will you sing at a particular place?"

The singer said, "Of course! As long as you pay me, I'll sing. I don't trust you, but if you give me the money beforehand, then I'll go wherever you want me to."

The two burglars gave the singer the promised sum of money and asked him to follow them. They brought him in front of a small bank and asked him to sing there. It was early evening, and there was only one guard watching this bank. As soon as the singer started singing, the guard fell asleep. Then the two burglars entered the bank and began collecting all the money.

After a while the singer stopped singing because the guard was fast asleep. He thought, "There is nobody to listen. This man doesn't like my music."

For a long time the singer waited for the burglars to come out of the bank. Finally he went inside and told them, "You've already given me my money. I'm leaving."

The burglars, greedily stuffing their pockets, said, "Go ahead," and they thanked him profusely.

As the singer was about to leave, all of a sudden he got the inspiration to start singing. Immediately both of the burglars fell asleep. In the meantime the guard who was outside woke up since he was not in earshot of the singing.

When the guard saw the singer coming out of the bank, he said, "What were you doing inside the bank? What's going on in there?"

The singer said, "I don't know," and he ran away.

When the guard went inside, he found the two burglars sleeping and he caught them.

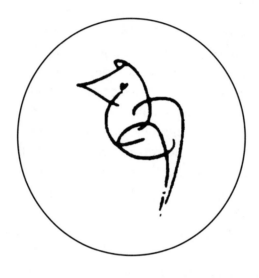

*Your life's prayer
Must unveil the truth.
Your heart's meditation
Must prevail over falsehood.*

The Thief's Protector

Two policemen were chasing a thief, but they couldn't catch him. Finally, the thief ran into a house and asked the owner for protection. He told the owner, "I'll give you half the money I stole if you protect me." The owner said, "I will definitely protect you, but you have to keep your promise."

It was evening, and the policemen had been 200 yards behind the thief and didn't see where he'd gone. When they came to the house where he was hiding, they asked the owner, "Did you see a thief come in here?"

The man said loudly, "Where? A thief in my neighborhood?" Then he started screaming, "Thief! Thief!" and the neighbors came out and joined the police in their search. The thief was not to be found anywhere; the police were ready to leave when the owner of the house said, "I believe the culprit will be caught. In God's creation, if anyone does anything wrong, he will be caught. How I hate thieves. We work hard for our money and then thieves come and steal it. Of all crimes, I hate theft the most."

Then everyone went home, including the policemen. The man went back into his house and told the thief, "Everyone's gone. I even joined the search party and I played my role well. Now give me half the money."

The thief said, "I have a new idea. From now on, I'll never tell a lie or have anything to do with anybody who tells lies. I hate liars. From now on if I see anyone telling lies, I'll punish that person. You're the first person I've seen telling lies."

The man exclaimed, "What? I saved you!"

The thief replied, "Yes, you told those people you did not see me. You protected me, but you lied. So you are the first person I've seen telling lies." Then the thief took out his revolver and said, "Now I'm going to kill you." The man started crying and the thief said, "Let me leave peacefully or allow me to kill you."

The owner said, "Go peacefully. I don't need your money. Just go."

*Inside a self-giving purity-heart
I see always
A thousand smiles shining
brightly.*

The King and the Traveler

One day a king said to his minister, "I don't really know what's happening in my kingdom. Unless I go about in disguise, I'll never know what my subjects are really thinking. People bow down to me and show respect, but I don't know their true nature. I want to discover the true nature of my subjects."

The minister said, "That is an excellent idea."

The king said, "This evening I'm going to walk around my kingdom and I would like you to accompany me. We will go about in disguise like ordinary men. No one will follow us. We'll go alone." The minister agreed.

That evening the king and the minister went out. As they walked along, they happened to see a traveler. The traveler said to them, "I'm exhausted. Are there any guest houses here where I can stay. I have no money."

The king said to him, "We don't know of any guest houses in our city."

The traveler exclaimed, "You don't have guest houses? What kind of place is this? If you were to come to my city, you'd easily find a place to stay!"

A middle-aged man was passing by and asked, "What is happening?" The man did not recognize the king at all.

The traveler said, "I'm from another town and I asked these two men if there is a guest house where I can take shelter tonight. They say there is no place. In my city, there are places to stay."

The man said, "These two are fools. They don't know

our kingdom. Our king is so kind and generous and he has made us so good that we don't need any special guest houses. All the houses serve as guest houses. If you come with me, you will see what a good host I am. Or, you can go to any house. These two are fools."

Then the man turned to the king and the minister and said, "You live here and don't know how kind and generous our king is? He'd be shocked if he heard that a traveler could find no shelter here. Perhaps you come from another city and that's why you don't know about our hospitality."

The king and the minister were totally silent. Finally the king said, "Can you tell us your name in case other people ask for shelter? That way we can recommend you. We've never known such a kindhearted man."

The man gave the king and minister his name and address and then brought the traveler with him to his house. The man kept his promise and treated the traveler quite well.

The following day the king summoned the man to his palace. When the soldiers arrived at his house to bring him to the palace, he was very frightened. "What have I done wrong?" he asked, trembling.

When the man reached the palace the king said to him, "I was sincerely moved by your kindness." The king told him the whole story and gave him a great sum of money. Then he said, "I'm ordering my workers to build many guest houses in my kingdom. I want my kingdom to be a place of hospitality. People should feel that I am truly generous. But until now I haven't provided shelter for visitors. You have opened my eyes. From now on we shall have guest houses for all the travelers."

*Since the beginning of creation
Self-giving and happiness
Have been oneness-friends.*

A Well of Wisdom

There was a miserly man whose wife was very generous. But the wife did not have access to her husband's money. They had so much money that they could easily have helped their village. For months people suffered from drought and famine. Because of the drought there was not enough food and people were dying of starvation. The wife begged the husband to dig some wells so that at least their neighbors could have water. But the husband did not want to spend money to dig wells.

The wife said, "Who knows, by digging in the ground, perhaps even I can find water."

So she asked their one servant to help her dig a well at a particular place. The wife herself, a respectable lady, joined the servant in digging. Every day they dug, but they found no water. The husband laughed and laughed and said, "Yes, you can dig for a year and there will still be nothing. Only the well of your stupidity is getting deeper."

One day the servant had a clever idea. He said, "Mother, we are working hard, but your husband is being so unkind and cruel. Let us play a trick."

"What kind of trick?" the wife asked.

The servant said, "Every morning your husband comes to laugh at us. Let's put some oil on the ground where we are digging. When he sees the oil, he will get very excited. He will employ many workers and servants, thinking we have found oil here. They will dig and, who knows, perhaps there will be some water here."

The following day the husband came and saw the oil on the ground. He was excited and said to himself, "I want to take credit for discovering this oil." Then he said to his wife and servant, "Will you do me a favor today? Can you bring me something from the market? I'll give you anything you want if you do me this favor."

They went to the market to buy what he requested. The wife was totally innocent; she had forgotten about the oil trick. In the meantime, the husband brought 20 workers to continue digging at the same place so that he could take credit for discovering oil. They worked for a few hours and finally hit water.

The workers were thrilled to find water, but the owner of the house was disappointed. He said, "Who wants water? I wanted oil so I could sell it and become richer. How can I sell water? I can only give it to my neighbors."

The wife and the servant came back from the market and were delighted to see the water. The husband said to them, "How can it be? This morning I saw oil on the ground. I hired workers to dig for it. This morning there was oil, but now there's only water."

The wife said, "Money and power surrender to the well of wisdom."

"What are you talking about?" asked the husband.

"This is a result of our servant's wisdom. We tried so hard to find water but we failed. Then he had a brilliant idea. He knows how miserly you are. He knew that if you saw oil on the ground where we were digging, then you would start digging for oil. God wanted you to help the needy. God didn't want you to become richer by discovering oil."

*Impossibility always bows
To humanity's
patience-mountain.*

Emptying the Sea

Once two partridges, a husband and wife, were going on a trip. Before they left, the wife laid some eggs near the ocean. Then the husband said to the sea, "We are going on a sea voyage. You must take care of these eggs for us. If we don't find the eggs when we return, we'll empty you."

The sea agreed to take care of the eggs, and it kept them safe. A few days later the two partridges came back, but they couldn't find the eggs. They screamed at the sea. The sea wanted to give them the eggs, but it couldn't find them. The birds cursed the sea; they began taking out a drop of water at a time and throwing it on the land.

"We are going to empty you," they said to the sea.

Some little birds saw all this and they asked, "What are you doing?"

The partridges replied, "We are punishing the sea because it didn't keep its promise to look after our eggs."

The little birds thought it was a noble task and they joined the partridges. After a while some big birds took up their cause. They also started taking out water drop by drop. This went on for weeks.

One day, Garuda (a divine bird who carries the great cosmic god Lord Vishnu) came and asked, "What are you doing?"

The birds said, "Can't you see? We are emptying the sea."

Garuda said, "You fools, how long will this take? You will never be able to do it. The sea is vast, infinite."

But the birds answered, "No, we have determination and perseverance."

Garuda was very surprised and said, "Let me show them Compassion. I'll ask Lord Vishnu to help them. If Vishnu helps, then certainly they will be able to find their eggs. If the eggs are still in good condition, Vishnu will be able to return them. But if they are destroyed, he can do nothing for them."

He went to Vishnu. "Vishnu, I have never seen fools like these. If you really care for fools, then will you do them a favor?" Garuda then told him the whole story.

Vishnu said, "No, they are not fools. They are showing the spirit of patience and perseverance. This is how human beings must try to empty the ignorance-sea, drop by drop. It is what seekers must and should do. The ignorance-sea is vast. If sincere seekers want to empty it and replace it with knowledge-light, then they must do it the same way, drop by drop. I am very pleased with these birds. I will command the sea to return the eggs."

Garuda said, "The sea wanted to give them the eggs but it misplaced them and believes they are destroyed."

Vishnu said, "I will use my psychic power to show the sea where they are."

He used his psychic power and the sea immediately found the eggs and returned them to the partridges. Then Vishnu said to the birds, "Perseverance, patience and self-giving all are of paramount importance to fulfill one's divine task."

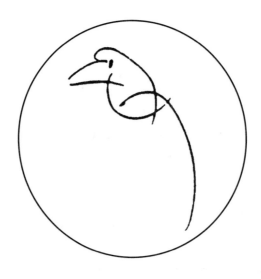

*Be affectionate and
compassionate.
Remember only thing:
Like you,
Everybody is desperately fighting
Against ignorance-night
In the battlefield of life.*

The Buddha's Message

There was a great king named Vindusar who ruled his kingdom wisely. When he died, his eldest son, Ashoka, ascended the throne. Ashoka's brothers were all handsome and strong, but Ashoka was not. His brothers constantly made fun of him because he was not good-looking.

When Ashoka became king he decided to take revenge, so when he got the throne, he killed his brothers one by one. Then he killed all his relatives who criticized him. He killed whoever spoke ill of him. He also wanted to be the lord of a vast kingdom, so he conquered a place called Kalinga, destroying many Buddhist temples and killing many Buddhists in the process.

One day he was in his fortified palace when he heard a pitiful crying. The relatives of the thousands of people whom he had killed were cursing him and lamenting and grieving for their dear ones. Ashoka felt sorry. Suddenly he heard a voice chanting, "*Buddham saranam gacchami*: I take refuge in Lord Buddha." Again and again he heard this voice chanting the same words. It was soothing. He thought of the Buddha's Compassion and felt that a change was taking place in his life, but he could not account for it.

When he went out into the streets, he saw one of the greatest followers of the Buddha, Upagupta, chanting nearby. Ashoka approached him and said, "Forgive me, but I heard someone chanting, and I wish to be initiated. I want to be a follower of the Lord Buddha."

Upagupta told him, "I was chanting." The king was deeply moved. Upagupta initiated him and he became Upagupta's disciple. After that, Ashoka took refuge in the Lord Buddha–in the Buddha's Compassion and in the Buddha's Light. He no longer paid attention to his kingdom or his throne. Eventually he became a religious mendicant, devoting his life to God. He put on an ochre cloth and roamed from place to place all over the world, chanting the Buddha's glory and establishing Buddhist temples. He opened up free hospitals for the poor and unreservedly gave things to the poor and the needy. He became compassion incarnate. Even his own daughter went to Sri Lanka to spread the Buddha's Light. Everywhere Ashoka went–even in mountain caves and on pillars–the Buddha's message was inscribed: "*Ahingsha parama dharma*: Nonviolence is the greatest virtue."

Sacrifice does not speak;
It only acts.
Its action is infinitely louder
Than a thunderbolt.

Babar's Sacrifice

The first Mogul Emperor Babar was a poet, a hunter and a man of wisdom. He often had to fight his enemies in order to maintain his own kingdom, but he had a good army and always won.

Babar had a son named Humayun, which means "fortunate." Sadly enough, a series of unfortunate events took place in Babar's and Humayun's lives.

When Humayun was 16 years old, his father wanted to conquer a particular place ruled by Ibrahim Lodi. The son said, "Father, you know our army is nothing in comparison to Ibrahim Lodi's army. How can you dare to fight with them?" But Babar replied, "No, my son, we shall conquer them. They may have the numbers, but we have the quality and the capacity."

The son said, "Father, I always abide by your will. Let's go."

Both the father and son were great heroes and with their small army they went to conquer Ibrahim Lodi's army. Surprisingly, they defeated the enemy. The people were very pleased with their new conquerors, for the old ruler had not been a good one. One of the local governors owned India's most precious diamond, which was called Kohinoor. The governor gave Kohinoor to Babar's son, Humayun, because of his bravery. Humayun showed it to his father and said, "Father, this is for you."

But Babar replied, "No, my son, you deserve it. You have got it and you should keep it. I am proud of you.

You fought bravely. That's why you have been given this diamond. Keep it. I will be happy if you do."

Father and son returned to their own kingdom. Alas, in a few hours' time Humayun fell ill. Day by day his condition grew worse. Many doctors tried to cure him, but none succeeded. They all agreed that his days were numbered. Many people prayed to Allah for Humayun's recovery, but to no avail.

Then a saint came to Babar and said, "If you make a great sacrifice, if you sacrifice something most precious, then your son will be cured."

Babar asked, "What kind of thing should I sacrifice?"

The saint said, "Give away Kohinoor. It is most precious."

But Babar said, "Kohinoor is my son's possession. What kind of sacrifice would that be? I have to sacrifice something of my own. I have so much wealth and property, and such a vast kingdom. But Kohinoor is not mine; therefore I cannot sacrifice it. Even if I did own Kohinoor, it would not be a real sacrifice to give it away. Even if I give away my wealth, power and kingdom, I don't think this is the most precious sacrifice I could make. My life alone is most precious. I am ready to give my life."

Then he walked around his son three times, praying to Allah, "The most precious thing I possess is my own life, so take my life instead of my son's. This is my only prayer."

To his surprise, after he completed three rounds, his son stood up completely well. But then Babar immediately fell deathly ill.

Humayun cried and said to Allah, "My father is going to die, but I shall eternally treasure my father's fondness for me and my father's implicit faith in Your Compassion."

Allah listened to the father's prayer, and in three months' time Babar died. This is the love that a human father can have for his son.

Do you want to know
Something incredible
But absolutely true?
The heart of the universe
Is your soulful smile.

Satyavama's Perfect Husband

When Satyavama reached the age for marriage, her parents wanted to find a husband for her. Satyavama said to them, "I will only marry a man who always listens to me. If I say sit down, he'll sit down. If I say stand up, he'll stand up. If I say eat, he'll eat. If I say run, he'll run. It has to be that kind of man; only then will I marry."

The parents said, "Who needs that kind of wife?"

Satyavama insisted, "If you don't find that kind of man for me, I won't marry."

Her parents pleaded with her. "We want you to get married. Now that you're grown-up, what will people think? It's not good to keep an unmarried girl at home."

Satyavama said, "I agree with you, and I'm ready to get married, but my husband has to be at my beck and call."

The parents looked everywhere for a husband for their daughter. They found many handsome and learned men who were willing to marry her. But then they were told, "There is one unfortunate thing. You have to be at her beck and call and always obey her."

The men would reply incredulously, "Obey her every command? That is servitude!"

Everyone became angry with the parents. Some laughed at them, some insulted them. "Why do you make this kind of proposal?" they asked. The parents were helpless. They couldn't find anyone to accept their daughter's proposal.

Then Krishna heard about the situation. He said, "I am the right man for her." So he went to their home and said,

"Satyavama, you are looking for a husband. Here I am."

Although Krishna already had a few wives, he said to Satyavama's parents, "If she wants a husband who will obey her, I am ready. If she wants me to do something, I am ready to be her perfect slave."

Satyavama was thrilled to accept Krishna as her husband. She had said that she would marry anybody who agreed to this proposal. Now, of all people, Krishna wanted to be her husband. He was venerated by everyone. Although Krishna had other wives and children, he married Satyavama.

As soon as they were married, Satyavama started telling Krishna, "Do this, do this, do this!" Whenever she asked him to do anything, he did it. But Krishna's smile conquered her. Each time he smiled, she would forget to give him a new job. "O Krishna, what am I going to do?" she said. "As soon as I see your face, as soon as I see your smile, I feel that it is I who have to listen to you. You are all love and joy. By asking you to do things, do I get any joy? Only by looking at your face do I get satisfaction."

Krishna said, "I knew it would be this way." So Krishna and Satyavama were very happy together.

A good heart has
The power of the sun
And
The beauty of the moon.

A good heart is
A special Grace of God
And
A special face of man.

The Cyclone

A middle-class couple from Calcutta was traveling to Europe on a large ship. After a few days, a cyclone came up suddenly and it began raining heavily. Many small boats capsized. The passengers in the large vessel raised a hue and cry because there was no way their lives could be saved from imminent catastrophe.

The wife said to her husband, "Everyone's crying because we know our lives can be counted in minutes. Why are you so calm and quiet? Don't you have any worries or anxieties? Don't you think that we will die in a few minutes? Why are you silent?"

On hearing this the man took a pistol from his pocket and aimed it at his wife. The wife said, "You're crazy. What are you doing? This is no time to make jokes."

The husband smiled broadly and said, "Look, you know that it's me, your husband, your dearest one, aiming this pistol at you. You know perfectly well that I won't kill you because of my tremendous love for you. God, who is the Author of all Good, is infinitely more compassionate than I am or than I ever could be, and we are His children. Do you think that He will allow us to be destroyed, or that He will destroy us? If I cannot kill you because of the little love that I have for you, how can God destroy us? He has infinite Love for His children, although we don't know and never will know how His Love and Compassion works in and through us. May God's Will be fulfilled in God's own Way. Today let us be observers, and tomorrow let us participate in the fulfillment of His Cosmic Will."

Immediately the cyclone stopped and everything became calm and quiet. The wife, proud of her husband's wisdom, fell at his feet.

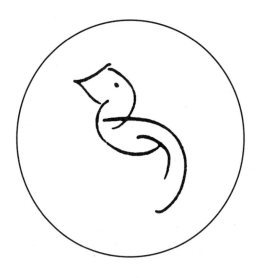

Oneness is the only need.
We can establish oneness
Only when we become
The soulful life of peace and
The fruitful heart of love.

Once You Realize God,
All the Cosmic Gods Become Yours

There was a great seeker whose name was Gyandas. A few times he had experienced a vision of his family's presiding deity, and this made him very happy. One day Gyandas and a group of seekers were praying together at the banks of the River Narmada. After some time a spiritual Master came and stood in front of them. He pointed to each one and remarked on their spiritual development. To some he said, "You are ripe, mature and advanced." To others he said, "You are unripe and immature; you are a beginner in the spiritual life."

Gyandas was one of the unfortunate ones. When it was his turn, the Master told him that he was an immature seeker. He could not believe his ears! He had always thought that he was truly advanced because he had a vision of his presiding deity a few times. He also felt that there were a few among those whom the Master had called forward who were not really advanced at all.

Poor Gyandas was miserable. He went home and prayed and cried the whole night. In the small hours of the morning he had a sweet dream. In the dream his presiding deity appeared. Gyandas asked her, "How is it that I am not advanced? You have been so kind to me. You have appeared before me a few times, and I thought you came to bless me because I am advanced in the spiritual life."

The deity said, "The spiritual Master was right. You are not advanced, but that doesn't mean that you will never be advanced in the spiritual life. You, too, can be a great spiritual Master like that Master, but you have to be initiated first.

"A Muslim mendicant has come to your village. Everybody thinks that he is a simple, ordinary mendicant, but he is a great spiritual Master. Let him initiate you."

The deity's words gave Gyandas the shock of his life. He said, "Initiation? I need initiation? And from a Muslim? He's filthy! He only takes a bath once a month. I can't go near him. He smells! I can't have him as my Master."

The deity said, "Then you will always remain unrealized. If you want to advance and become spiritually mature, if you want to have boundless peace and joy, then go to him for initiation."

For a long time that morning the seeker argued with himself. Finally he decided to go to the Muslim teacher. He went and stood before him with bitter anger, inner disgust, pride and, at the same time, terrible fear. Then he saw something which puzzled and confused him to no end. The Muslim Master was lying down by the banks of the River Narmada with his feet on a wooden statue of Lord Shiva!

Gyandas said to himself, "Look at this villain! How dare he place his feet on our cosmic Lord Shiva! Lord Shiva is one of our Trinity! He is deliberately insulting me because he knows I am a Hindu." To the Muslim Master, Gyandas said, "I will never become your disciple!" He was furious.

The Muslim Master said to Gyandas, "My boy, I have not come into your life to confuse you. I know what you are thinking. Now do me a favor. Remove this wooden statue of your Lord Shiva. Place it wherever you want to."

Gyandas grabbed the statue and placed it quite a distance away. But to his amazement, the statue started walk-

ing like a human being and went back under the feet of
the Muslim Master. Gyandas was astonished and shocked
at the same time.

The Muslim Master said, "Come, you hold the statue
and let me go away." Gyandas held the statue while the
Muslim Master walked about 200 yards and then stood
still. The seeker felt compelled to bring the statue to the
Master, but he argued with himself. He said, "No, I won't
go!" He felt a terrible pressure from within and also an
inner command from the statue itself to go to the Muslim
Master. But he repeated to himself, "I won't go to him. I
won't accept him as my Master."

Gyandas put the statue on the ground, and the statue
quickly ran to the Master. So once again the Master lay
with the statue at his feet.

What could Gyandas do? He was puzzled. He thought,
"If I don't take initiation from this Muslim Master, then I
will never realize God. But this man is deliberately insulting my Hindu God. I must at least ask him why he is
doing this to me."

Gyandas went to the Muslim teacher. Before he could
open his mouth, the Master said, "I will remove all your
confusion and illumine you. Once you realize God, the
cosmic gods become yours. For a God-realized person,
the cosmic gods are like parts of one's own body. It is not
beneath my dignity for my hands to touch my feet. Again,
I can also touch my head if I want to. I can touch any part
of my body with any other part. There is no question of
superiority or inferiority, for all parts of my body belong
to me.

"Each limb of my body I claim as my own. In the same
way I claim Shiva as part of my existence. For Shiva to be
at my feet is like one part of my body touching another

part. Shiva and I are one.

"Realize God. Then you will see that there is neither superiority nor inferiority. We are all one. Stay with me and I will initiate you. Once you are initiated, you will go back to the other spiritual Master and hear from him that you are far more advanced than all the other seekers who were with you yesterday."

*Spirituality is
truth-awareness.
Spirituality is
life-emancipation.
Spirituality is
oneness-manifestation.*

A Blossoming Goodness

There was once a great Indian spiritual leader, Swami Vivekananda. His earlier name was Narendranath. His nickname was Bilé. During his childhood and adolescent years he was extremely divine, but also very mischievous. His parents, especially his mother, sometimes puzzled and worried over him.

She would say, "O Lord Shiva, I have prayed to you to grant me a son like you. But instead of coming into my life, you have sent me your ghost. He is nothing but a ghost, my Bilé, always breaking things and creating problems for me. How long can I tolerate his endless mischief?"

But there were also quite a few good qualities that Bilé's mother also saw in him, so inwardly she was satisfied. But outwardly she told everyone, "My Bilé is so notorious!"

One day, when he was only five years old, Bilé saw a few Indian hookahs, or smoking pipes, in the living room. One was for the Brahmins (the priestly Hindu caste), one for the Kshatriyas (the warrior Hindu caste) and one for the Muslims. He tasted each one, and to his surprise discovered that all the hookahs tasted the same.

Alas, he was caught by his own father. "What are you doing, my Bilé?" he asked.

Bilé replied, "Father, I was just examining the smoking pipes. I thought that the one for the Brahmins would be better than the one for the Kshatriyas, because Brahmins are great. And the Muslims are heroic and spirited, so I thought that the Muslim pipe would be special. But they are all the same. No one pipe is superior to another."

Bilé's parents were shocked. "Why have you started smoking at such a tender age?" they asked. "And listen to what you are saying!"

Then his mother said, "My son, you're too spoiled. You've become too smart. Come here." The child came to the mother and she took him upstairs to his room and closed the door.

Two hours later, the maid came running to the mother, screaming: "Bilé is throwing away all his clothes. He's throwing everything he has in his room out the window! There are beggars below grabbing his garments as they fall. And he is so very happy!"

At this the mother ran upstairs and demanded of her son, "What's the matter with you, Bilé?

The boy replied, "Mother, we're so rich. We have whatever we want, whenever we want. But these are poor people. They have nothing. If we don't give to them, then who will give to them? We have more than enough; so my heart wants to give these things away. They need them more than I do."

His mother's heart was full of joy and delight. She embraced her son and shed tears of delight that his heart was so sympathetic, so vast and so self-giving, and that he had so much oneness with the poor and with the Supreme Pilot in all.

*To complete
The golden dream of peace,
Selflessly serve
And unconditionally love.*

The Sannyasin in America

Swami Vivekananda, a great Indian hero, and a great spiritual renunciate or *sannyasin*, came to America to preach spiritual philosophy and to offer India's message to the nation. After addressing the World's Parliament of Religions held in Chicago in 1893, he became famous overnight.

This lofty spiritual figure had many friends and admirers. One day, some of these friends and admirers came to his house to ask him questions about Indian philosophy and spirituality. They were moved by his answers. By the time they departed, it was nearly midnight.

After they had gone, the man thought of India, his poor India, especially Mother Bengal. He said to himself, "I am going to bed. But tonight there are thousands and thousands of people without beds who will be lying in the street, poverty stricken. Here I have got a cozy and most comfortable bed. But once upon a time, I was a renunciate. Even now I am a renunciate. I used to roam in the street with no food, with nothing. Still, from time to time, I have no food or clothes. I'm in a destitute condition.

"God blesses me with riches, and my friends keep me in their homes. They've even given me this beautiful apartment. Indeed, I'm living in great luxury. In a few minutes, I'll go to sleep in a comfortable bed, and yet many of my fellow brothers and sisters in Bengal will be sleeping in the street.

"My heart bleeds for them. I have not fulfilled my task.

I must help my poor Indian brothers. I must save their lives; I have to enlighten them, to awaken their consciousness. There is so much to do! Alas, what am I doing here? I need rest, but I won't sleep on the couch. I'll sleep on the floor."

He unwrapped his turban and laid it out on the floor for bedding. Early the following morning when the owner of the apartment, who was his friend, came to invite him to breakfast, he saw this great Indian hero lying on the floor. He said, "What is the matter?"

The Indian replied, "Thousands and thousands of my brothers and sisters spend the night in the streets. How can I sleep in a comfortable bed? I can't, unless and until I have done something for them. It is my duty to serve God in the poor and needy. So the life of comfort is not for me. The life of selfless service, the life of dedicated, devoted service, is for me. Service is my goal, service is my perfection in life."

Only one thing to learn in life:
You must think of yourself
The way God thinks of you—
As another God.

A Swami Smokes with an Untouchable

Swami Vivekananda enjoyed smoking. In the days of his pilgrimage, when he walked the streets of India, smoking was his great avocation.

One evening as Vivekananda was walking along a village street in northern India, he came to a small cottage where an old man was smoking an Indian hookah. Vivekananda had a tremendous desire to smoke, and asked the old man if he would share his pipe.

The man said, "Swami, I'm a scavenger, I'm an untouchable. How can I share my hookah with you? You can't smoke with an untouchable. I'm so happy to see you; you are so handsome, so spirited. But, alas, I come from an untouchable family."

Vivekananda felt sorry that the old man was an untouchable. He said to him, "I'm sorry. You're right. I can't smoke with you." Vivekananda left him and continued walking.

But he felt miserable. He said to himself, "What am I doing? What have I done? Didn't my Master, Sri Ramakrishna, teach me that wherever there is a human being, there is also God? Each human being embodies God. I learned this from my Master.

"I've given up everything; I'm a renunciate. I'm one with the rest of the world by virtue of my renunciation, and still I preserve this sense of discrimination. Here is a cobbler, a scavenger; and here I am–a man of the highest caste together with a man of low caste. Low caste, high caste!

How can I have the heart to distinguish? Are they not all God's children? This artificial separation, this idea of superiority and inferiority: how can I have this kind of feeling?"

Vivekananda then went running back to the old man and said, "Please, share your hookah with me. Each man is God Himself."

The old man fearfully gave the hookah to the Swami. He smoked to his heart's content and then said to the old man, "I am divinely happy, supremely happy, for two reasons: My human desire is fulfilled I am able to smoke; and my divine desire is fulfilled because I have been able to realize my inner vision of universal oneness. My Supreme Lord abides in all. I have been able to manifest this vision of mine today by sharing your hookah with you today.

"God is for all. He is not only for me, but for all. I see Him in each individual. My only goal is to please Him unconditionally. I'll be ever grateful to you, for it is through you that my Lord has taught me the supreme lesson: that we are all one, we are all equal, we are all children of our Absolute Lord Supreme."

My mind's suspicion-night
Is a binding chain around
nothing.
My heart's wisdom-light
Is a loving chain around
everything
That I unmistakably have
and eternally am.

She Lends Money with Wisdom

There was a very rich man who was extremely cruel and miserly. His wife was kindhearted and affectionate, and full of sympathy for everyone. No one liked the husband, but everyone liked the wife. However, she thought, "God gave me this bad husband, so what can I do? Nobody likes him, so at least I should." She was kind to him and served him day and night.

A famine struck the region where they lived, and many villagers came to them for help. The wife gave money to everyone and showered them with affection and sympathy. Her husband did not mind her generosity, in spite of his miserliness. He said, "As long as I don't have to personally give, I'm satisfied."

When she gave money to the people, they said, "We're only borrowing this money. We'll pay you back."

She said, "No. You don't have to pay it back. It's a gift. Just take it."

They refused, saying, "No. We'll repay you when the famine is over."

She said, "If you really want to repay me, then give me the money the day my husband dies."

Some people were shocked to hear her talk like this. Others thought that when her husband died, she would have many expenses for the funeral and that was why she said this.

One of their sons happened to be present when his mother made this odd statement. The son loved both parents dearly, but when he heard what she said, he was angry. He went to his father and told him, "Mother is asking people to repay the money she's giving them after your death."

The father could not believe this. "How can she say this? She always gives money freely, so why is she now asking them to return the money and why does it have to be after my death?"

The husband went to the wife and asked her, "Tell me why you're asking people to return the money after I die?"

She said, "You don't understand. You see, people don't like you. They hate you. Everybody wants you to die today, but many people have taken lots of money from me, and by nature people don't want to pay it back. From now on, instead of thinking of your death, they will pray to God to keep you alive so that they don't have to pay it back. I want you to live for many, many years. Who knows? One day you may also become very affectionate, kindhearted and sympathetic.

"I played a trick. I want them to pray to God every day that you live. This will make me happy. Who cares for the money? I want you to live for a very long time." The husband was extremely touched by his wife's wisdom and love for him and he vowed to be more compassionate toward others.

For ages
Humanity has been trying
to find joy
By dividing reality
And analyzing the pieces.
When will humanity learn
That joy can be found
Only in oneness?

Enough of the Mind

There was a great scientist named Dr. Satyendranath Bose. His was a truly immortal name in the scientific world, not only in India but in other countries as well. Some people are great, but are not good. Dr. Bose was both great and good. His heart was the heart of a child. He had a special fondness for children and played games with them. One game that he liked particularly was called Karam. He was a fine player and, though he had distinguished himself as an eminent scientist, he enjoyed playing with the children and they, for their part, accepted him as their hero.

One day he happened to be playing Karam with some children, and was deeply absorbed in the game. A middle-aged man came by and watched the game. After a while the scientist asked him, "What can I do for you?" The man replied, "I would be grateful if you would preside over a meeting we're holding at our school tomorrow."

Very politely the scientist responded, "No, I can't. I'm sorry. You'll have to find someone else."

But the visitor urged, "We need you badly. No one else will do. And we'd be deeply honored if you'd preside over the meeting."

With utmost politeness the scientist repeated, "I can't come tomorrow at that time because I am supposed to play here with my friends. Nothing gives me greater joy than to play with children. I have presided over hundreds and hundreds of meetings, and they don't give me any joy. I want joy, you want joy, everyone wants to be happy. To me, Karam is infinitely more meaningful than presiding over a meeting, for I know that intellectual and argumentative people will be there, and they will bring their reasoning minds. I am fed up with reasoning minds. I want only the heart, the sincere and pure heart. I find that kind of heart here, with my little friends.

"I promised them I'd play with them tomorrow, and that's what I'm going to do. I want to remain in the heart. I have played in the mind and now I am playing in my heart. Satisfaction is there, only there. Peace is there, only there."

With God's Grace
We begin.
With God's Encouragement
We continue.

Tagore Sings

There was once a talented little boy, Rabindranath Tagore, who was very beautiful to look at and also very smart. His father was rich and well-respected; he owned vast plots of land and had many servants. The boy spent most of his time with the servants. He was the youngest in the family and the servants all adored him.

One day, he was singing a song he had composed. The song expressed the idea that, "The eye cannot see You, although You are inside the eye. The heart cannot know You, although You are inside the heart." He was singing it most soulfully, and the tune was hauntingly beautiful.

The father heard him singing from another room and was deeply moved. He asked his servants to go and bring the little boy to him. Then the father said to his youngest son, "Can you sing the song for me again?"

The boy didn't often get the opportunity to come to his father because his father was always very busy. So although it was a great honor that his father had called him, he was also afraid of his father.

The father said, "I'm your father. Don't be shy. Just sing your song, my child."

The boy sang and the father was so deeply moved that he went into trance. When his trance ended, the father entered his office and wrote the boy a check for 500 rupees. In those days, 500 rupees for a child was really something. When he gave it to the boy, he said, "In the past, the Mogul Emperors honored talented people with gifts. The Mogul Emperors are no more, but your talent is so remarkable that you deserve that kind of honor."

His son was excited and delighted. He ran and showed the check to his servants. The servants lifted him up into the air. They were so proud that their little hero had become such a great poet.

Eventually, Tagore became India's greatest poet and won the Nobel Prize. He composed some 1,800 songs, many of which are sung all over India, including India's national anthem, "Jana Gana." Truly, Rabindranath Tagore was a creative genius who excelled in every field of the arts. In the latter part of his life he even took up painting. As poet, singer and playwright, he won love and respect not only in India but all over the world.

He remains in the vanguard of poets for his lyrics, songs, plays and stories. India's Tagore will remain eternally unique. In 1961, on his birthday, the whole world observed his centenary.

Love your family much;
This is your great duty.
Love mankind more;
This is your greater duty.
Love God most;
This is your greatest duty,
The duty supreme.

The Brahmin and the Old Woman

One day a high-class Brahmin (a person from the Hindu priest caste) went to the Ganges for a swim. This man also held the esteemed position of judge of the Calcutta High Court. He was a great scholar and pundit. His name was Sri Durudas Banujee. On that particular day he was supposed to go to court, and he was late. So he could not spend as much time as usual bathing in the Ganges. After taking a quick dip, he was on his way back home when all of a sudden he heard someone say, "Hello, hello, can you spare a moment?" It was an elderly woman. The Brahmin said, "Yes."

The woman said, "My house priest could not come today and there is no one to conduct our daily house prayers. My daily house prayers can't be performed without a Brahmin. You're a Brahmin; will you do me a favor? Will you come and do the prayers? Our house deity will be displeased if he is not worshiped today. Please come." So the Brahmin said to the old lady, "Yes, I'll come." And he followed her to her house.

He was well-educated, a great scholar who knew Sanskrit and the scriptures far better than the Brahmin who usually conducted her prayers. He did everything. It took him more than an hour. After he was finished, the lady said to him, "I wish to reward you. I'd like to give you something for the prayer ceremony. I'll pay your fee, and I'd like you to take some coconuts and bananas."

The Brahmin said, "No I can't take anything."

"Please, you have to take this," the old lady said. "You've done me a great favor; please accept money and fruits for your prayers."

But the man said, "No, I can't do it. I'm happy I was able to help you, but I can't accept a fee." Then he left hurriedly.

The lady didn't know who he was, and he never told her of the important position he held. Even though he held such a high post, he still regarded his duty to other people as supreme.

*The heart of every human being
Can leave behind a legacy
Of world-illumining
compassion.*

The Patriot and the Hooligan Chief

There was a great patriot who conquered everyone's heart in India, especially the Bengalis. He was known as the leader of great leaders. When he was in college he was a brilliant student. He had always had a fondness for spiritual people. He helped the poor, the sick and the needy whenever he could.

Once when he was a young man, cholera broke out in Calcutta and the rich people left the city. When the epidemic broke out, there was no medical treatment for the poor, so he went to the poorest section of town and treated the sick.

There were many hooligans in that part of town. They threatened him and said, "Don't come here and bother us. We don't want you. You're well-educated and come from a rich family, while we are poor and ignorant. Leave us alone." Bravely, he replied, "Do whatever you want. If you want to kill me, kill me. I've come into the world to help the poor and sick. I'll continue to bring money and food and try to help as much as I can."

One day the only son of the hooligan leader was stricken with cholera. So the young man went to his house and cared for the son, feeding him and giving him medical treatment. The hooligan leader was deeply moved. "I threatened you and warned you not to come here, and still you come to help my own son. You're a brave man."

The young man said, "It's not a matter of bravery; it's a matter of necessity. I see God in everyone. When I see someone suffering, I feel it is my duty to help. One must help one's brother when he is in need."

The hooligan chief bowed down to the young man and said, "You're not human. You are divine."

This matchless leader and patriot was none other than Netaji Subhas Chandra Bose.

You can be happy
Only when you ask God how
things can be done
In God's own Way.

The Tragedy of Dasharatha

There was a great king named Dasharatha. King Dash-aratha was an expert archer, and his teacher, Bhargava, was pleased with his student. There was, however, one particular skill that Bhargava didn't impart to his student. It was a special type of archery in which it is not necessary to even see the prey. By just hearing the sound of the animal, no matter where it is, the archer can shoot it. Bhargava did not want to give this secret knowledge to Dasharatha because he was from the warrior caste. Although people from the warrior caste are spirited, courageous and determined, they have one weakness: they lack a disciplined life and sometimes fall victim to restlessness. Therefore, Bhargava was unwilling to give Dasharatha this special skill.

But Dasharatha begged and begged his teacher. Repeatedly he declared, "I won't misuse it, I promise you."

Finally, Bhargava acceded to the king's entreaty. "All right," he said, "I will teach you. But I'm afraid one day you'll bring serious calamity to yourself, to the members of your family and to some innocent victims through your improper use of this knowledge." So reluctantly Bhargava taught the secret skill to Dasharatha.

Dasharatha was delighted and proud, for he knew that he had now mastered all the strategies of archery.

A few years passed and Dasharatha didn't even consider using the special skill that he had been taught. But one day, a strong desire entered into his mind. He thought, "Let me go into the forest and test the skill Bhargava has given me. Then I'll know whether I actually have learned how to kill animals without seeing them."

So Dasharatha went into the forest. When evening came, a sound reached his ears, which he was sure was an elephant trumpeting. Dasharatha immediately pulled back his bow and let the arrow fly. Then lo and behold, a human sound came to him in the night: "Mother, Mother, I am hurt."

Dasharatha followed the sound to its source and found a young boy, about nine years old, bleeding heavily from the wound the arrow had inflicted in his chest. He had come to fetch water from a pond. He body was doubled over in pain, but he was still clutching the water pail in his tiny hand. The little boy's father, a great sage, was blind. His mother loved her only child dearly. Because his parents were old the son helped them in many ways, even at this early age. This particular evening his parents had been thirsty, so he had come to draw water from a pond near their cottage. As he was approaching the pond, the arrow came flying towards his heart and struck him down.

When Dasharatha came and saw the scene, he was terrified at what he had done. He cried out piteously, "O, Guru Bhargava, you were right! I was not meant for this sacred knowledge."

The little boy turned his eyes to Dasharatha and said to him, "I am dying. Please do not feel sorry for me. I know that we must all die someday. But do me a favor, please? Will you take this pail of water to my parents? They are thirsty and expect me at home. Please, please do me this small favor. Don't worry about me. This is my fate, but please go and give water to my parents." Then the little boy, who said his name was Sindhu, turned his face to Heaven and died.

Dasharatha burst into tears. With one hand he took up the dead body of the little boy and with the other he carried the pail, full to the brim. Slowly, and with a heavy heart, he made his way to the cottage of Sindhu's parents.

When Sindhu's father heard the sound of footsteps he said, "Sindhu, Sindhu, my Sindhu, you have come! We've been waiting for you. What makes you so late, my child? Both your mother and I are pinched with thirst, and you have come to quench it. You're our dearest child, our only darling. Please, try always to be prompt. Don't waste time on errands that take you away from us. We need you every moment."

Dasharatha could remain silent no longer. He said, "Oh sage, I'm the wretched Dasharatha. Forgive me, forgive me. Your child, Sindhu, is no more. I've brought him home. But, alas, he's without life. Although I'm the king, I'm entirely at your mercy. Do what you want with my life."

The father and mother could not believe their ears. As soon as the mother saw her son lying dead in Dasharatha's arms, she fainted and immediately her husband followed her. In an hour's time, when they had both recovered, they said to Dasharatha, "King, please do us the kindness of building a pyre right away. This is our last request: as soon as the pyre is lit, we wish to join our son on it. When the fire is blazing, we'll place our son on it, and then we shall enter the climbing flames."

In great distress, the king said, "No, no! You can't do that! I am already responsible for one death! I can't bear two more. Please forgive me, and I'll do anything in my power to console you, but this thing I can't do."

With one voice the parents answered him. "No, king, we can't stay. We won't be dissuaded from joining our son. He was dearer to us than life itself. Without him our lives are meaningless. Let us join him."

"Then," Dasharatha said, "what will be my punishment?"

"No punishment," the mother replied. "Why should we blame you? This is our fate. We forgive you. Our son forgave you and so do we."

Her husband, the sage, said, "Wait! Our son has forgiven him, and you may forgive him, but I can't. Although I have practiced yoga and other austerities all my life, I can't forgive him.

"Dasharatha, you are responsible, totally responsible, for our son's death and I curse you. You too, will one day lose your son the way I have lost mine. You'll be obliged to send him into the forest because of your foolish fondness for one of your wives and, as a result, you'll lose him."

At the time of these events, Dasharatha didn't have a son. But when he heard the curse he cried out, "O God, don't give me a son. I don't need one. It is better not to have a son and not to miss him than to send one into the forest. But I cannot conceive how this could take place. How could it happen? Why would it happen? Who among my wives would be so cruel as to compel me to send my son into the forest? Impossible, impossible! Yet the curse of the sage might come true. O God, I beg You, either give me a son who will escape this curse or give me no son at all. For to lose a son and enjoy the kingdom would be impossible. O Lord Supreme, forgive me, forgive my misdeed. Let this curse remain unfulfilled, I pray."

But, alas, how can the curse of a great sage pass unfulfilled? There came a time when Dasharatha was indeed compelled by his second wife to send his son, who was dearer than the dearest, into the forest. When his son was gone, it was simply impossible for Dasharatha to bear the shock of his son's exile and, lamenting the loss, he died.

Today's failure-plants
Will tomorrow grow into
Success-trees.
Patience from below
And compassion from above
Can and will do the impossible
Easily.

Patience Illumines

$\mathcal{T}$wo sisters were both married to the sage Kashyapa. Their names were Kadru and Binate, and they were extremely fond of each other. Once, Kashyapa left for a few days of serious meditation. While he was away, the two sisters were talking, and they entered into a serious dispute over the color of the cosmic god Indra's elephant. Binate said it was white, while Kadru said it was black. Each was so certain of being right that both agreed that whoever was wrong would become the slave of the other.

Kadru, who had three sons, asked them about that particular elephant. "You have seen Indra's elephant so many times. Can you tell me its color?"

The sons said, "Yes Mother, it is white, pure white, like the moon."

Kadru cried out, "O God, what have I done? Now I have to become my sister's slave! Save me! Please, save me!"

"How can we help you?" they asked. "Why did you make such a stupid promise? We're sorry, and we will feel miserable when you become Mother Binate's maid, but we're helpless."

"You're not helpless," Kadru said. "Do me a favor. Tomorrow morning Indra's elephant will come to the lake. You and a few friends must wear black garments and carry black pieces of cloth with you. Then, when the elephant starts approaching, cover it with the cloth. When Binate and I come to see it, it will appear to be black."

Early in the morning while it was still nearly dark, the

elephant came to the lake. Binate saw the pieces of cloth in front of the elephant. "Yes, it is black," she cried out. "I've lost!"

Kadru said, "Now you must be my slave, my maid-servant, for life."

When Kashyapa returned from his few days of medita-tion, he saw that Binate had become Kadru's slave and was miserable. Kashyapa himself felt terrible. "How could this happen?" he asked.

When Kashyapa heard all about it, he said to Binate, "Kadru's sons have deceived you. The elephant is white."

Binate could not believe her ears. "I'm sad to hear that Kadru and her sons have deceived me. But it's too late now. I've committed myself to being her slave. A promise is a promise."

Kashyapa said, "Binate, you should have had more patience and waited for the elephant to come nearer. Then you would have discovered their trick and not com-mitted yourself to be her slave forever."

Binate cried, "What can I do now?"

"Wait for the hour." Kashyapa consoled her. "Although it's unfair, be patient. One day you will also have sons. Your children will either take revenge or do something to illumine Kadru and her sons and make the family happy again."

In three or four years Binate was blessed with a child, but the birth was premature. Binate was distressed: "Is this the result of my patience?" she cried. "To have a premature child? This child is supposed to save me. It's impossible." In her anger she kicked the child and he became deformed.

"What have I done?" she screamed.

Again Kashyapa consoled her. "You should have had more faith in my prophecy. It will one day prove true.

Have patience: wait and see. Your sons will save you."

"I don't need more children," she said. "I'm ready to remain a slave to my sister."

When her son was still very young, he said to Binate, "Mother, I understand why you kicked me; you were mad with grief. Don't torture yourself over what you've done, and don't be sad that you've become your sister's slave. You were very happy once, and now you are miserable. But a time will come when you will be free from this bondage."

Two years later, Binate was blessed with another child, Arun, who was very spiritual. Binate was happy with her new son.

Kashyapa said, "He will really help you."

Indeed, the brightness of the child frightened and tortured Kadru and her children, and they were terribly jealous of him. As Arun grew older, his illumination compelled Kadru's sons to surrender, and they began leading a divine life.

One day Binate said to her son, "Arun, I know you have the power to compel my sister to free me from my promise. But please, let your older brother be cured by you instead. I'm content to remain a slave."

But his older brother said to Arun, "No, I'm content to remain deformed. Let my mother be freed. You must not save me; save her."

Arun replied, "There is no reason why you, Mother, should remain a slave. My stepbrothers have become divine. Kadru, too, is ready to receive illumination."

Very soon, Kadru freed Binate from her old promise, and again the two sisters became close. Their children also became very fond of each other, and in a short time the oldest son of Binate was cured.

Kashyapa said, "Because of your patience, Binate, one of your sons has freed you, as I predicted. He has transformed and illumined Kadru and her sons. You lost the feeling of oneness over an elephant. But the past is dust. Now let us again enjoy the oneness of a family."

Immediately Indra's elephant appeared outside Kashyapa's home, and his two wives gratefully said: "O Kashyapa, great sage, we clearly see now that you have shown us that patience illumines and oneness lives in the heart of God's creation."

*Alas, what I have
Is a greedy mind.
And what I am
Is a starving heart.*

The Golden Swan

The Buddha told this story as something that took place in one of his previous incarnations. At that time, he was a simple man with a wife and three daughters. He was always kind to people and was dearly loved by his family. When he died and entered into the soul's world, he observed what was happening on earth. He was distressed to see that his family was poverty stricken.

So he returned to his family as a beautiful golden swan and said to his wife, "I've come back to you in this form. Once a month I'll come and leave one of my gold feathers for you to sell. In this way you will be able to meet with your expenses."

So every month he came and left a golden feather.

The wife was very happy, and the daughters were delighted when they saw their father. The swan would stay for a few minutes and then leave.

One day an idea entered the wife's mind: "My husband may not come regularly, or he may change his mind and stop coming, or he may grow old and die. The best thing is for me to catch him and strangle him the next time he comes, so that I can have all his feathers."

The daughters were shocked: "How can you even think this kind of thing, Mother?"

The wife said, "All right, I won't strangle him. But I will pluck all his feathers. If he can't fly anymore, no harm. You will take care of your father."

The daughters pleaded with their mother, "Please, we

love him deeply. He's kind to us. He could have stayed in the soul's world, but he comes in the form of a swan to help. Look at his love for us."

But the mother wouldn't listen. The next time the bird came, she caught him by the neck and plucked his feathers, one by one.

It was painful to the swan and he cried and screamed pitifully: "What are you doing? I've been good to you!"

When she was finished, the bird was in pain and could not fly. Then all of a sudden the golden feathers turned into ordinary white feathers. The greedy wife was miserable and the daughters were smitten with grief. But what could they do? Their mother was so cruel.

Then the mother went into her room and opened the box where she'd been keeping the gold feathers that she had accumulated. She knew there were enough gold feathers to meet her family's expenses for at least six months. But when she opened the box, she found that these feathers, too, had turned into ordinary white feathers; they were no longer gold.

The three daughters fed the poor swan each day and showed him love and affection. The mother was helpless. "This happened because of my greed," she said to herself.

The daughters said to her, "Look what you've done! Even if he hadn't come for six months or a year, we could have lived comfortably on the feathers that you'd saved. Now father doesn't have golden feathers anymore."

The father said, "This is our fate."

Slowly and steadily the swan's feathers grew back again, but this time they were pure white, and finally the bird was able to fly away. The children were happy that he was free. Now he could be happy.

The mother was miserable, not because the bird had

gone away, but because her stupidity led her back to a life
of poverty.

When you consciously use time
To do something divine,
You enter into timeless Time.

When you are consciously
thinking
Of something divine,
eternal Life comes
And shakes hands with you.

The Conqueror of Time and Space

Shyama Charan Lahiri was an Indian spiritual Master who worked as an office clerk. One week he noticed that his boss, who was an Englishman, was sad and distressed. Lahiri asked what was troubling him. The boss told him his wife was very ill in a hospital in England, and that he had not heard any news from her or from her family.

Lahiri suggested, "Let me go into the next room and meditate. Then I'll bring you news." The boss smiled at the young clerk. While he appreciated his good will, he didn't have any real faith in him. He believed that to do this kind of thing, one had to be a great spiritual Master with exceptional occult power. And he knew Lahiri only as a humble young clerk.

Fifteen minutes passed and Lahiri came out of the room and said to his boss, "In two or three days you'll receive a letter from your wife. She's doing well. You don't need to worry." He even related the contents of the letter to his boss.

In three days a letter did arrive, and its contents were exactly what the clerk had said they would be. But the story doesn't end here. A few months later the boss's wife came to India. One day she visited her husband's office. When she saw Lahiri, her eyes opened wide in surprise. She said to her husband, "How is it this man is here? I saw him near my deathbed in the hospital. He looked at me and smiled, and then I recovered." Her husband and all those who were working in the office were taken aback.

Commentary:

A spiritual Master is one who has solved space and time problems as well as all other human problems. In his oneness with God's Cosmic Will, the length and breadth of the world abides. He doesn't go anywhere; he's simply there when he's needed. Medical power is often uncertain. But spiritual power is uncertain only when it's unaware of the omniscient capacity of the Source. When spirituality is fully aware of the capacity of the Source, and its surrender gradually gains the capacity of the Source, lo and behold, it is blessed by the Source and grows into the all-powerful Source itself.

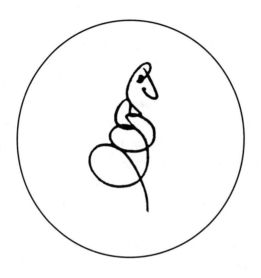

When the power of love
Replaces the love of power,
Man will have a new name:
God.

The Art of Photography Surrenders

Shyama Charan Lahiri was dead-set against anyone photographing him. But since his close disciples repeatedly requested permission to take his picture, he finally agreed. When the photographer arrived the Master asked him many questions. The photographer was deeply honored, so he explained the basics of photography.

When it was time for the Master's picture to be taken, the photographer could not see him in the viewfinder. He aimed the camera at the Master, but saw nothing. When he focused on others, he saw them perfectly, but when he focused on Lahiri, there was nothing visible.

Finally the frustrated photographer said to the Master, "It's impossible. I can't take your picture."

The Master smiled and said, "All right, I'll behave myself. Now you can take it." This time Lahiri was clearly visible, and he snapped the picture. Then Lahiri said to him, "Spirituality and spiritual power far surpass modern science. Have faith in the Real, which is spirituality."

Commentary:

Some spiritual Masters are not in favor of picture-taking. They feel that since the body is transient, we should pay no attention to it. There are other Masters who are of the opinion that a photograph doesn't merely represent an object, but can serve as an inspirational force and an elevating and illumining experience. These Masters feel the supreme necessity of seeing the highest reality first in the body, and then transforming the body into the soul's universal mis-

*sion and transcendental vision. According to them, a pho-
tograph is not a mere piece of paper reflecting an outer face
or appearance; it is a revelation of what one inwardly is.*

*There are those who think the achievements of the world,
in the world, are useless, and the world itself is useless, for
it is unreal; therefore, they do not want to leave behind
anything when they leave the earthly life. But for those who
think of the world as the field of God, manifestation will
strive to leave behind a transformed life and revelations of
an immortal soul. Both parties are correct in their
approaches to reality according to the depth and height of
their own realization.*

How can you be hopeless?
I am growing in you
With my ever-luminous
And ever-fulfilling Dream.

How can you be helpless?
I am inside you
As infinite Power.

The Master's Spiritual Power

Śri Yukteshwar was a dedicated disciple of Shyama Charan Lahiri. One day his dearest friend, Ram, was stricken with cholera. Two doctors tried to save his life, but it seemed that all their efforts were in vain. Both were certain that Ram would die in a matter of hours.

Yukteshwar ran to his Master, begging him to save his friend's life. Lahiri said to Yukteshwar, "You have doctors. Why do you need me? The doctors will save him. They can do what's needed without me."

Yukteshwar went back full of hope, but gradually his friend's condition worsened. When it was certain he would die in a few minutes, Ram said to his friend, "I'll be dead soon. Please tell the Master I have a last wish. It is that he come and touch my body and bless me." In a few minutes he was gone.

Crying, Yukteshwar went back again to Lahiri in order to give him Ram's message. The Master said, "How is Ram?"

Yukteshwar replied, "Go see for yourself. His last prayer was for you to touch his dead body and bless him."

But Shyama Charan said, "Then why should I go? He's not dead."

"Yes he is," said Yukteshwar. The doctors have confirmed it."

Lahiri took some oil from a lamp and said, "Go put this oil in his mouth."

His friend was dead, but this was the command of the Master, so what else could Yukteshwar do? He went and put the oil into Ram's mouth. In a few minutes Ram came to life, saying he had a dream in which he saw Lahiri in a beautiful form. The Master said to him, "Ram, why are you sleeping? Get up and come to me."

Then Ram stood up, put on his clothes and both the friends went to Lahiri's house. The Master said to Yukteshwar, "I've taught you how to conquer death. From now on if anyone dies, just put a small quantity of oil in his mouth. I've given you the medicine to conquer death." Everyone laughed. They knew perfectly well that the oil was just an outer gesture, a token, a symbol. The Master used oil only to convince the physical mind with a physical object. The actual gift of life had come from Lahiri.

Commentary:

It is only the omnipotent spirituality that can turn impossibility into possibility. But spirituality, out of sheer magnanimity, tries to work through worldly means to convince the physical mind that the principles of truth are accessible to the human in us.

*We must think of ourselves
As a most beautiful bird
Flying inside Infinity's, Eternity's
And Immortality's heart-sky.*

The Call from the World Beyond

Shyama Charan Lahiri was extremely sick and was in his bed. His intimate disciples surrounded him as he explained some of his favorite verses from the Bhagavad Gita, the most sacred book of the Hindus. All of a sudden he stood up and said, "What am I doing here? Why am I wasting time? It is high time for me to go to my real home."

A few hours later, three of his intimate disciples at different places saw his luminous spiritual body. He had come to console them. They didn't know of his passing; they knew only that he was sick. But when they went to their Master's ashram (spiritual community), they found that he had died. His physical body was dead, but he had visited them in his spiritual body.

When the soul-bird flies out of the body-cage, it can be visible only to those who want to see it. At that time, the limitations of the body disappear and the infinite expansion of the soul appears. When a sincere seeker enters ignorance-life, he says to himself, "What am I doing here?" When the same seeker enters into the aspiration-life, he says to himself, "Why don't I stay here all the time?" Our earthly home embodies the desire-life; our heavenly home embodies the illumination-life.

With physical courage
We take pride
In breaking the world
In our own way.

With the courage of the spirit
We offer the world to God.
We place the world, our world,
At the Feet of God
So that He may guide and mold
our world,
In His own Way.

A Citadel of Strength

There was a time when hooligans tortured the people of Bengal. They informed the residents of certain houses that they were going to rob them, and then they did in fact rob them. They molested the women, tortured the maids, stole what money they could and caused tremendous damage. Consequently, many rich people left the city while many others who could not leave lived in a state of constant anxiety.

One day the hooligans informed a particular family that they were going to plunder their home. The maids of the house were scared to death. Some of them decided to leave the house; others couldn't make up their minds. Finally they all decided that they would leave and allow the hooligans to take whatever they wanted. But at that moment, a young boy in the family who was only 12 years old, said, "No! I won't go. The rest of you can go. But they won't take anything, I assure you."

His uncle was thoroughly surprised. He exclaimed, "Oh, so you're a hero! You'll stay and they'll kill you!"

The boy said, "I won't be killed. But you go. I have some friends who are experts in stick arts and they will fight the hooligans."

The uncle said, "Don't be a fool."

"No, uncle," the boy pleaded, "give me a chance. I won't be harmed, and I assure you, nothing will be stolen."

"All right then, my child. Proceed with your plan," replied the uncle.

So the boy brought his friends, who knew the art of self-defense, as well as how to attack people with their sticks.

When the hooligans came there was a terrible fight. Many people were severely injured, but nobody was killed. In the end the hooligans were badly defeated, all because of the tremendous inner strength that this young boy possessed.

Eventually this valiant young boy became the literary emperor of Bengal: Bankim Chandra Chatterji. His remarkable courage, patriotic fervor, seer-vision and inspiration-flood aroused the great subcontinent of India.

*The Infinite has
cheerfully embraced
The finite
So that mortals can successfully
grow into
The Immortal.*

Bankim Chandra's Only Medicine

After the age of 50, Bankim Chandra Chatterji's health began to fail. There were still many books he wanted to write, but alas, his poor health made writing difficult. The members of his family became alarmed that he wasn't taking the medicine his doctor had prescribed.

One day the doctor came to him and said, "What can I do? You don't take your medicine. Don't you want to live? Many people will be saddened if you die. You're a great man, a hero and leader of Bengal. If you don't take your medicine, how will they fare? How will they go on living? You are the father of the nation, and if you leave, many will feel fatherless. Granted, you have a frail constitution, but in that frail constitution India has seen a reservoir of stupendous possibility."

Bankim Chandra said, "Who said I don't take medicine?"

"Where's your medicine? Show me," said the doctor.

Bankim Chandra picked up a copy of India's most sacred scripture, the Bhagavad Gita, from the table and showed it to the doctor. "This is my medicine, my only medicine. Your medicine may cure my body, but this will cure my body, vital mind, heart and soul. This medicine will make me immortal; there is no other medicine that can do that."

The doctor remained silent.

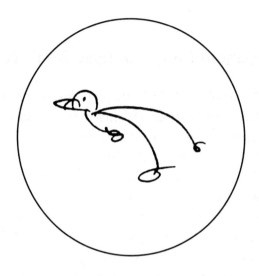

Love is the secret of oneness.
Sacrifice is the strength
of oneness.

Gandhi Buri's Supreme Sacrifice

In the time of the British rule of India, there once lived an extremely patriotic woman. She was a great admirer of the distinguished Indian leader Mahatma Gandhi; his very name was for her a sea of inspiration. Despite the fact that she was 73 years old, she did many patriotic things that inspired the people of India in the hope of getting the British out of the country. Because of this woman's admiration for Mahatma Gandhi people called her Gandhi Buri, "buri" meaning "old lady."

In 1942, Mahatma Gandhi was arrested, and all of India was furious. Around the nation, people held processions, and shouted the slogan "Quit India," which was Mahatma Gandhi's message to the British government. The day after Gandhi's arrest, Gandhi Buri was involved in a march to a police station. The people in the procession wanted to pull down the British flag from over the police station and hoist up the Indian flag in its place.

The police stood in the way and warned the protesters that if they came forward, they would be shot.

All the marchers stopped except Gandhi Buri. She snatched India's flag from one of the young boys in the procession and ran toward the building. At first the police laughed at her. "Enough," they cried! "No more! Get out of here old woman. We don't want to kill you."

But Gandhi Buri cried, "Kill me. I'm not afraid. I want to free my Mother India."

She ran toward the staircase that led to the top of the

police station. Before she reached the stairs the police shot her. She was still holding the flag in her right hand as she chanted the slogan of the Indian independence movement, *"Bande Mataram, Bande Mataram, Bande Mataram"*: Mother, I bow to thee. Then she died.

This old woman was so courageous that she gave her life for her country. From that day on, people who were in that procession dedicated their lives to the freedom of India.

The nature of divine friendship:
If one friend loses,
The other's oneness-heart will
break.
If one friend wins,
The other's oneness-heart will
make him feel
It is he who has won.

I Love You More Than My Own Life

There was a young boy named Ramesh, whose parents were not only rich, but also very kind. Ramesh was a good student. He studied each day from nine o'clock in the morning until noon. From noon to one he had recess, and then he studied again from one to three.

The students brought food from home to eat during the lunch hour. One day Ramesh realized that his friend Gopal had not eaten anything for lunch for a few days. As a matter of fact, Gopal wasn't bringing any food to school with him.

Ramesh went to his friend and asked why he was not eating anything. Gopal said, "My mother could not give me anything. She said we had nothing at home."

Ramesh said, "Don't worry. I will share with you."

"No, I can't take your food," said Gopal.

"Of course you can," insisted Ramesh. "My parents give me much more food than I need." Finally Gopal agreed, and for a few weeks the two boys shared Ramesh's lunch.

Then one day Gopal stopped coming to school. Ramesh was concerned. When he asked the teacher why his friend had quit coming to school, the teacher told him, "He comes from a poor family. His parents can't afford to pay tuition."

Ramesh was sad for his friend. When school was over, he got Gopal's address from his teacher and went to his house. Ramesh begged his friend to come back to school, saying that he would ask his parents to pay the tuition.

Gopal's parents were deeply moved by his kindness, and Gopal returned to school. Gopal's father was an old man. In a few years' time he died. When he died, the family became totally poverty stricken, and Ramesh supported them with his own money. When Gopal's sister was stricken with a serious disease, the family couldn't afford the hospital bills. Again Ramesh helped them out. In every way he was the friend and guardian of Gopal's family.

Both Ramesh and Gopal completed high school and went to college. One day Gopal said to Ramesh, "To say that my heart is filled with gratitude to you is an understatement. I love you more than I love my own life."

Ramesh said, "My friend, if you love me, that is more than enough for me. You do not have to love me more than your own life."

Gopal said, "But I do, and I want to prove it." Then he opened his penknife and cut his arm open. He began to bleed. Then he placed a few drops of his blood at Ramesh's feet.

Ramesh said, "What are you doing?" He touched the cut on Gopal's arm, placed a few drops of blood near his heart and said, "This is the place for your lifeblood. I give you my earthly treasure in the form of material wealth. You give me your heart's love, which is heavenly wealth beyond all measure."

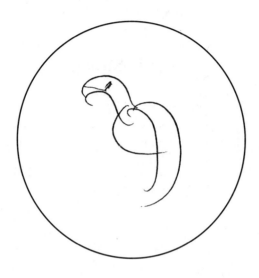

Devotion is the secret of secrets.
It lets you establish
The sweetest and the most
intimate
Connection with God,
Who belongs entirely to you.

Who Is Stronger?

There was once a great devotee of Lord Vishnu, a spiritual singer and poet named Surdas. Surdas was blind from infancy. He had six brothers who died fighting in a battle against the Muslims. Although Surdas was totally blind, he went in search of his brothers' bodies. While searching, he fell into a dry well.

For six days Surdas was trapped in the well. During this time he repeated the name of Krishna, the Avatar of Lord Vishnu, over and over again. Finally, Lord Vishnu appeared and lifted Surdas out of the well. He also restored Surdas' vision.

For a few days Surdas was extremely happy. Then his happiness began to fade because he saw that the world is full of ugliness and that people are always quarreling and fighting with each other. Finally he said to Lord Vishnu, "I don't want to see anymore. Please take my vision away again. When I couldn't see human ignorance so vividly, I was content. Make me blind so that I can be happy again." Lord Vishnu granted his prayer, and once again Surdas was blind.

Surdas composed soulful songs. Since he had many good friends and relatives, there was always someone who was kind enough to write down the words and music for him. One day, when he was greatly inspired, he began calling out for one of his stenographers, but no one was available. Suddenly Surdas felt someone's presence. "Who's there?" he asked, "Announce yourself." There was no answer. Since

Surdas was sure of someone's presence, he reached out, but whoever was there vanished from his grasp.

Surdas said, "I know, my Lord, it is You who have come to me. You have the power to snatch Yourself from my grasp. You are physically stronger than I am. But let's see if You are spiritually stronger than my heart. Let's see if, even for a fleeting second, You can disappear from my heart. This is my challenge. I'm sure that You will not be able to leave my heart even for a fleeting second."

Surdas was right. Lord Vishnu could not escape from the loving heart of his devotee.

What powerfully you hold
In your thought-world
Will make you either
A street beggar
Or a great king.

The King and the Sage

Once there was a king who was always fighting. One day he was badly wounded in a battle. A sage passed by and touched him, and the king was cured. He wanted to give the sage a reward for saving him, but the sage didn't want anything.

The king said, "I don't want to be indebted to you."

The sage said, "In the future I'll ask for something. I don't need anything now, but one day I'll come."

Months passed and the sage was praying to God one day for peace, light and bliss, when a desire entered his mind. For the past few months his cow had not been producing milk. "She's old," he said. "I'll ask the king for a new cow."

He went to see the king and found him in a temple. He was praying for more wealth and more fame.

The sage said to himself, "I won't ask him for a cow. He's a beggar like me." And he turned to leave.

The king stopped him and said, "Sage, you saved my life. Please tell me what you want. I'll give you anything."

The sage said, "I pray to God and meditate. He is all I need. I don't want to take anything from anyone in need. You told me you took an oath that you would not be indebted to anyone. I, too, have taken an oath. My oath is that if anyone is in need, then I won't take anything from that person. That's why I won't take anything from you. You're praying to God for material things. You're begging for God to give you wealth and fame. So how can I ask

anything of you? God has shown me that everyone is a
beggar. So if I need something, I'll get it from Him."

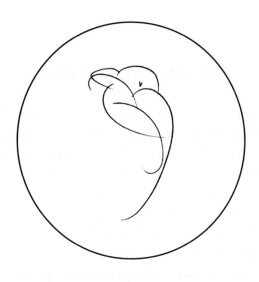

*We try to possess and
bind the world,
And while we are doing this
We see that we have already
been bound
And are possessed by the world.*

The Burglar's Signature

Once there were two kings who were good friends. They helped each other in times of need. One day one of the kings needed a large sum of money. He asked his friend for a loan, and his friend immediately agreed to give him the money he needed. The first king said, "I'll send my minister to you; please give it to him." The other king agreed. So the first king sent his minister and three body-guards to the other king's palace.

There was a notorious burglar in the first king's realm who stole money every night. He was a real rogue, but no one could catch him. He had stolen lots of money and used it to bribe certain palace officials to give him news of what was happening there. He hoped one day he would be able to enter into the palace with their help and steal everything.

The thief heard from his palace friends that the minister was going to get money from the other king. That evening, as the minister and three guards set out from the palace, the burglar and three of his friends came and surrounded them. The thief said, "Give us your clothes. I've brought other clothes for you. I'll wear the minister's clothes and my three friends will wear the guards' uniforms." Then the thief and his followers forced the minister and the guards to exchange their clothes.

The thief did not know how to read or write but he was very clever. Several days earlier, he had gone to a great scholar and asked him how to write the minister's name.

The scholar asked him, "Why do you have to know how to write the minister's name?"

The thief replied, "I have my reasons."

The scholar said, "No, I won't do it."

Finally the burglar threatened, "You will or I'll kill you."

This frightened the scholar and he acceded, "Please don't kill me. I'll teach you how to sign his name."

The burglar wanted to be able to sign the minister's name in case the other king asked for his signature on a receipt. He knew that he was going to get the minister's clothes, so he also wanted to be able to sign the minister's name.

After changing clothes the thief and his three followers went to the neighboring king's palace for the money. The burglar wanted to show off that he knew how to sign the minister's name, so he said, "Don't you need my signature?"

The king said, "Oh no, your king and I are good friends. I trust you."

But the thief was feeling cocky. "Still, it's good to get the signature." he said.

The king said, "All right, if you want to sign, you can."

So the false minister wrote down "Junga the Burglar."

The king was shocked. He thought to himself, "How can this be?" He asked the minister and three guards to wait for a while. Then he ordered his guards to go to the other king.

When they arrived, the guards said to the King, "We understand that Junga is the most notorious burglar in your kingdom. How is it that your minister has signed Junga's name? Is your minister making fun of our king?"

Just then the real minister entered the palace. He told his king that he had been forced to change clothes.

Immediately the king sent the message to his friend, who arrested Junga. Then he personally delivered the money.

So the thief was caught because of the scholar's cleverness and Junga's arrogance. Since Junga was illiterate, the scholar taught him how to write his own name and told him it was the minister's name. He knew that Junga, being a boastful man, would try to show off his new skill. The scholar hoped that in this way, Junga could be captured.

Every day
Try to hasten the completion
Of your God-ordained task:
The transformation
Of earth-bound sorrow
Into Heaven-free joy.

The Hooligan's Son

Once there was a hooligan who was destroying the peace and joy of an entire kingdom. The king was miserable because he wanted only peace, joy and harmony in his kingdom. The king's soldiers tried to capture this hooligan, but they always failed.

The hooligan's wife had committed suicide because her husband would not give up stealing. At first the hooligan was miserable because he had lost his wife, but even then he would not stop stealing. The only other member left in his family was his little three-year-old son, his only child.

The king, distressed over the situation the hooligan had caused, said, "Since everyone else is failing, I'll try to catch the culprit myself." So one night he disguised himself as a thief, broke into the hooligan's house and kidnapped his son.

When the hooligan returned home the following day and saw that his only son was missing, his heart was completely broken. He said, "My wife warned me not to continue this kind of life, but I didn't listen to her. Now my only child is gone. What's the use of continuing to steal and torture people?"

So the hooligan became a mendicant and began leading a very simple, ascetic life. He thought of his wife and child often, especially the child. He kept asking himself, "Who could have kidnapped my only son? I don't have the heart or the energy to try to find him again. Whoever has stolen him will never return him to me." He continued to lead a very pure and pious life, and in six months he was totally changed.

Meanwhile, the king raised the child in his palace. He had a son the same age and he showed both of them the same love and affection. One day both boys fell ill and no physician could cure them. As a last resort one of the court physicians said, "I know of an herb that will cure them. It's very difficult to procure, but I'll try."

In the meantime, the hooligan-turned-ascetic happened to come near the palace to pray and meditate for his illumination. Someone reported to the king that a saint was praying and meditating nearby. The king said, "I need the prayer of a saint. Ask him to come in and I'll beg him to help me."

So, at the request of the king, the saint came to the palace. His consciousness had changed so much that no one recognized him as the former hooligan. The king told him, "I have two little children. Both are dying. Would you kindly come to see them and pray to God for their recovery? I will give you whatever you want."

The saint said, "I will pray to God to save them, but I want nothing from you."

The king took him into a private chamber and showed him the children. The hooligan did not recognize his son because the child had received such good care. He was clean and well-nourished and, even though he was sick, looked completely different.

The doctor came into the room and told the king, "I have the herb, but there's only enough for one child. Who cares for the other child! Let your child be cured."

The king said, "No, I can't do that. If we have only enough for one child, please give it to the other one."

"Why?" the ascetic asked.

The king said, "Although he is not my child, I want him to be cured. Like me, his father has a heart. I stole his child. I know his heart is broken because he's lost his son. But I had no alternative. His father was a notorious criminal; a thief and a murderer. He was destroying my entire kingdom. When I kidnapped his son, inwardly the man was destroyed. He hasn't been seen since. This was the only way I could put an end to my kingdom's suffering. But I will never forgive myself if I allow his child to die, since I have already killed his father's spirit."

The king turned to the physician and said, "Give the medicine to the other child and allow my child to die. I hope that one day the hooligan will find his son. If he gives up his profession, then I will gladly go myself to return his son."

The ascetic immediately fell down at the feet of the king and would not get up. "What is the matter?" the king asked.

The ascetic said, "My king, I am the hooligan and this is my child. I caused so much trouble for your subjects. I deserved your punishment. Today you've proved what kind of heart you have. Please keep my son. I promise I'll never steal again. I've already taken to an ascetic life, but if you want, you can throw me out of your kingdom or kill me."

The king said, "You have changed your ways and are living a spiritual life. I will gladly take care of your child and I'd like you to remain here as my court sage. I am grateful that you came to pray and meditate for the recovery of the boys."

Miraculously both sons were cured and together the former hooligan and the king shed tears of gratitude.

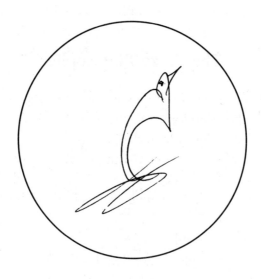

A genius is he
Who ends rules and regulations.
A genius is he
Who is nothing but a powerful
drop
In the ocean of cosmic
life-energy.

The Crazy Philosopher

Once there was a philosopher who was very well-known in the kingdom. On the one hand, he was very wise and everyone admired him. On the other hand, at times he seemed to be crazy. But people forgave his craziness because of his inner wisdom. They saw only his good side. The king cared for men of wisdom, so he liked the philosopher. He knew that sometimes people who are geniuses can act a little crazy.

One day the philosopher left his house for good. At night he slept in a cave and during the day he roamed the streets trying to avoid people. Those who could get near him asked, "Why do you always roam around alone?"

The philosopher answered, "I keep to myself for a simple reason: because you people are all dishonest. I'm looking for an honest man. You may be friendly but you're not honest."

Everyone was shocked at the philosopher's rude behavior, for each considered himself an honest person. But the philosopher said, "I myself am not honest, but I'm looking for an honest man."

One day a court officer brought the philosopher before the king and informed him, "Today a thief stole something. My fellow officer and I chased him and arrested him. As we were bringing him to jail we passed this crazy philosopher. He said to us, 'Two big thieves have caught a little thief.'"

The angry officer said to the king, "He called us thieves! How dare he!"

The king looked at the officer and then at the philosopher. He thought for a few seconds and then he said, "He's right. We're all dishonest."

Then the king said, "If I were not the king, I would give up everything and live the same kind of life that this man is living. I would live a simple life and I, too, would search for an honest person on earth. I'm king, but even for me honesty is something beyond my imagination. No matter how hard one tries to be honest, it is extremely difficult. He is looking for honesty in others. I would have tried much more sincerely to be honest had I not been king."

A falsehood-loving man
Is helplessly attached
To his unfulfilled desires.

A truth-loving man
Is sleeplessly devoted
To his unmanifested dreams.

Gandhi Passes His Own Examination

Gandhi never told a lie. Once the inspector visited his school class and gave a few words of dictation. The third word was "kettle." Gandhi's friends were able to spell the word properly, but Gandhi didn't know how.

The inspector began going around to check each student's paper. While the inspector moved from student to student, the teacher saw that Gandhi's spelling was wrong, so he touched Gandhi's leg with his foot to get his attention. With his eyes he urged Gandhi to look at someone else's paper. But Gandhi didn't want to copy from anyone.

When the inspector came to Gandhi, he said, "Here's a mistake. This boy doesn't know how to spell 'kettle.' He has written it 'ketle'."

The inspector wasn't angry, but he was disappointed that Gandhi didn't know the answer.

The teacher was very angry with Gandhi. "I told you to look at your friend's paper, but you wouldn't listen to me. You're a disgrace to my class."

Gandhi said, "I may be a disgrace, but I can't tell a lie."

Gandhi was sorry he'd made a mistake and had displeased his teacher, but he had pleased himself by being honest.

The teacher was silent.

*If you have
the sincerity-courage
To declare that you are weak,
Then God has
the Compassion-Capacity
To make you strong.*

Gandhi's Matchless Sincerity

A friend of Gandhi's needed money and asked if he could help him. At first Gandhi said, "I have no money." Then he conceded, "All right, I'll see what I can do."

Gandhi stole a piece of gold from his brother and sold it. Then he gave the money to his friend. Afterwards, he felt miserable for having stolen something.

He always told his father everything. He kept no secrets from him. Although his father was very sick and bedridden, Gandhi wrote him a note, saying, "I stole a piece of gold and I feel sad and miserable. Please forgive me."

When his father read the note, he got up from his bed. Gandhi was afraid he was going to strike him. But there were tears in his father's eyes. Then Gandhi thought that his father was disappointed in him for having stolen something from his own brother, and that made him feel even more miserable. Finally, his father tore up the note and tears flooded his eyes.

Gandhi assured his father, "Father, I'll never steal again. This is my first and last time. Please don't cry."

His father was deeply moved. "I'm crying, son, not because you stole something, but because of your sincerity. You're always so truthful. I've never known anyone as sincere as you. I'm proud of you."

Do not be afraid of tasting
The bitterness of failure.
Be brave!
The sweetness of success
Will before long befriend you.

Gandhi's Ashram

After he left Africa and returned to India, Mahatma Gandhi opened up an ashram at the request of close friends. The immediate members of his family and a few friends went to live there. They led a very simple, pious life, and prayed and meditated. The ashram was supported by rich merchants who often came to visit.

One day, Gandhi received a letter from a schoolteacher. The letter read: "I'd be grateful if you'd allow me to stay at your ashram with my wife and child. I'll do anything you want." At the end of the letter the teacher wrote, "Only one thing I hesitate to tell you, but I must: I'm an untouchable."

When Gandhi read this, he buried his head in his hands, "O God, I love the untouchables, for they are God's children. But my family will be furious. How can I welcome this man into the ashram? On the other hand, how can I refuse him?"

Gandhi spoke to the members of his family about the matter, and they were very understanding. "If you want to have this man here, invite him to join us," they said.

Still Gandhi hesitated. "The merchants who support the ashram are fanatics. They will worry about what society will think." Then he declared, "It doesn't matter. I'll allow this teacher to work and live here at the ashram."

The untouchable came to the ashram. As soon as the merchants found out, they stopped giving money to Gandhi. They said, "You're ruining society. You come from a good family, a good caste. How can you do this kind of thing? We won't support such an unthinkable thing."

Gandhi told them, "All right, don't give us money. But if somebody sincerely and soulfully wants to serve this ashram, I will allow him. Untouchables are God's children too."

Soon Gandhi ran into financial difficulty. One day, while walking along the street, he saw a merchant with a carriage. The merchant approached him and said, "I'm one of the merchants who used to support your ashram. Since you let an untouchable in, I haven't been able to help you because I'm afraid of what my friends might say. But my heart is one with you, and I want to give you money secretly. Please promise me you'll never tell anyone about this." Gandhi promised.

The merchant said, "Come here tomorrow and I'll give you a donation."

Gandhi returned the next day and the merchant gave him the money he had promised. Gandhi didn't even know the man's name, since many merchants had helped his ashram and he didn't know all of them personally. Gandhi asked his name, but the merchant wouldn't tell him. "Please," the merchant said, "I can't give you my name. Yours is a noble cause and I fully agree with you. But I have to live in society, so this must remain a secret. You're doing the right thing; therefore, I'm supporting your cause. But it's not necessary for you to know my name."

On that day, Gandhi's fate changed.

Each devoted moment
Prepares a beautiful sunrise
And a fruitful sunset.

Laosen Does the Impossible

There was once a king named Karnasen who was a great hero. For many years he and his sons defeated all his enemies in battle, but eventually he lost to a more powerful king. Karnasen lost his wife, his hero-sons and all his dear ones. He himself would have been killed by his opponent, but that king showed compassion. He said, "You're an old man. I don't want to kill you. I killed your wife and sons and all your relatives. I've destroyed your army. Go peacefully on your way."

Karnasen felt miserable. Since none of his family remained, he went to another kingdom and took shelter there. The king of that particular kingdom, whose name was Gaur, was kind to him and showered him with hospitality. He invited Karnasen to spend the rest of his life there. One day King Gaur said to Karnasen, "If you want to marry, I'll ask one of my sisters-in-law to marry you."

Karnasen said, "I'm an old man. Why should I start another family at this age?"

But King Gaur replied, "It will make you happy. It's good to have some near and dear ones."

Karnasen finally agreed, and soon he married Ranjabati. At that time Kripan, Ranjabati's brother, was away from the kingdom. When he returned and heard that his sister had married without his knowledge, especially to someone who was now a beggar, he became furious. Kripan was also jealous because King Gaur was showing Karnasen considerable affection and love. Kripan had hoped that he would be the closest one to the King, but now he saw that Karnasen was becoming close. He could not insult King Gaur, but he wanted to punish Karnasen.

Karnasen and his wife lived together for a number of years, but unfortunately Ranjabati was not blessed with a child. One day, in public, Kripan said to her, "You're a useless woman. You're a barren field!"

Poor Ranjabati felt miserable. She prayed to the sun god to grant her a child. Finally the sun god listened to her prayer and she had a son. The parents named him Laosen.

Laosen was a beautiful child. From early on he showed tremendous physical strength, and he became a great wrestler. He could defeat three or four wrestlers at a time. Laosen even used to fight tigers and whales. Now Kripan, Laosen's maternal uncle, was once again jealous. First he had been jealous of Karnasen because he was getting so much attention from King Gaur. Now he was jealous of Karnasen's son because he had become so powerful.

Kripan tried to kill Laosen. Once he hired ruffians to kill him. Another time he cleverly invited his brother-in-law and nephew to visit him so that he could honor them, and then he put two mad elephants along the route to kill his so-called guests.

One day Kripan became so desperately angry that he said to King Gaur, "I'll leave the kingdom unless you banish Laosen."

King Gaur said, "How can I, and why should I? Laosen is unconquerable. I'm happy he's a relative of mine. If anyone attacks us, he'll be able to defeat the enemy."

Kripan said, "Do you think that he can defeat anyone?"

The King said, "He is unconquerable. No one can defeat him."

Kripan said, "Can he do the impossible?"

King Gaur said, "There is nothing on earth that Laosen cannot do."

"All right, I'll believe it if he can compel the sun to rise in the west."

King Gaur said rashly, "I'm sure he can do even that."

Kripan was delighted to hear this. He knew that Laosen would not succeed.

When Laosen heard of this, he went to the king. King Gaur was very fond of Laosen's father and proud of Laosen. But now he was worried. He believed Laosen could do anything because he had so much faith in the young man. But he couldn't help feeling that it was impossible to make the sun rise in the west.

Laosen said to the king, "Don't worry. If you made the promise, I'll fulfill it." Then Laosen started praying to the sun god as his mother had done many years before. Soon the sun god came to him and said, "Keep praying. I'll see if it can be done. Just pray, pray, pray."

So Laosen kept praying. Meanwhile, his maternal uncle was very happy. Kripan was sure the sun would never rise in the west. He said to King Gaur, "Laosen can't fulfill your promise, so you'll have to fulfill my desire. He has to leave the kingdom."

King Gaur said, "Give him more time. He said he would do it."

Laosen prayed and prayed. One of his maids said to him, "Don't worry. The sun will be pleased with you someday."

Laosen said, "I've been praying a long time. I'm afraid he'll never grant me this boon."

Then the maid said to him, "Offer your life and he'll be pleased with you."

Laosen said, "If I die, and if the sun still does not rise in the west, I won't be able to do anything more. But if the sun god agrees to fulfill my desire, then I'm ready to die."

The maid said, "No, do it now. He will be pleased with you."

So Laosen chopped off his own head and immediately the sun god appeared. He brought Laosen back to life and said, "I'm truly pleased with you. I'll fulfill your desire. Tomorrow the world will see me appear in the west. Go tell King Gaur and your father."

Laosen was filled with joy. He ran to tell his father and King Gaur. Both of them, as always, believed him. Then King Gaur told Kripan, "Tomorrow morning you'll see that Laosen has really done the impossible."

Kripan said, "Tomorrow morning! You have committed to a time. If he doesn't make the sun rise in the west tomorrow morning, then you have to throw him out of the kingdom."

King Gaur said, "Yes, but he'll do it."

Kripan was the first person to disbelieve it, and the following morning he got up long before anybody else to see the sunrise. Much to his amazement the sun did rise in the west. Then the sun god appeared before everyone and said to Kripan, "You've caused much suffering for Karnasen and his son Laosen. Laosen is my devotee, and you've tortured him for many years. You deserve to be punished. From now to the end of your life you'll suffer from leprosy." This was the worst possible punishment he could have given.

Then King Gaur asked the sun god, "How could you do it? How could you rise in the west?"

The sun god said, "Is there anything that I won't do for my true devotee? If someone were to insult me and say, 'Sun, you must always rise in the east. Obviously you can't appear in the west; you don't have the power,' immediately I would agree. I would say, 'You're right. I can't do it!' But my devotee is dearer to me than my life itself. When he accepts a challenge, I also accept it. Kripan could have challenged me personally, but had he done it, I wouldn't have taken the trouble of breaking the cosmic law. But he challenged my true devotee. And Laosen was ready to sacrifice his own life in order to keep his promise.

"You can defeat me, but not my devotee. A true devotee can always do the impossible. God Himself may not want to do a particular thing; there is no need for Him to show the world that for Him nothing is impossible. But God wants to show the world there is someone who can do everything, and that is His true devotee. So don't challenge a devotee. You will always lose."

*The heart of every human being
Can leave behind a legacy
Of world-illumining compassion.*

Sympathetic Oneness

A father and son were walking together, enjoying the early morning breeze. They had covered a good distance when the father stopped suddenly and said, "Son, stop!"

The son said, "What's wrong?"

The father said, "Nothing in particular, but let's not walk any farther on this road."

"Why not?" asked the son.

"Do you see that elderly man coming toward us?" the father asked, pointing down the road.

"Yes, I see him," replied the son.

"He's a friend of mine," said the father. "He borrowed money from me and can't pay it back. Each time he sees me he tells me he'll borrow the money from someone else and give it to me. This has been going on for a long time, and I don't want to embarrass him anymore."

The son said, "Father, if you don't want to embarrass him, why don't you tell him that the money is a gift and you don't want it back?"

"I've already told him that," said the father. "When I said, 'I don't want it back; it's a gift,' he got mad. He said, 'I'm not a beggar. I'm your friend. When I was in need, you gave me money, and when I can, I'll give it back. I want to remain your friend, not become a beggar.' Now I don't want to embarrass him, and I don't want to be embarrassed myself. So let's take another road."

The son said, "Father, you are truly good. I'm very proud of you. It's usually the borrower who tries to avoid the lender. It's usually the receiver who is embarrassed, not the giver. But you want to spare him embarrassment. What I have learned from you is a sympathetic oneness."

*A supremely peace-flooded
Oneness-heart
Knows no limits.*

I Want Only One Student: The Heart

There was a spiritual Master who had hundreds of followers and disciples. He often gave discourses at different places—churches, synagogues, temples, schools and universities. For over 20 years, whenever he was invited, and wherever his disciples made arrangements for him, he gave talks. He gave talks for children and for adults. He gave talks for university students and for housewives. Sometimes he gave talks before scholars and advanced seekers.

Finally there came a time when the Master decided to discontinue his lectures. He told his disciples, "Enough! I've done this for a long time. I won't give any more talks. From now on I will be silent."

For 10 years the Master gave no talks. He maintained silence in his ashram. He maintained silence everywhere. He'd answered thousands of questions but now he didn't even meditate before the public. His disciples begged him to resume his previous practice of giving talks, answering questions and holding public meditations. They all pleaded with him, and finally he consented.

Immediately the disciples made arrangements. They put advertisements in the newspapers and put up posters everywhere to announce that their Master was going to give talks and hold high meditations for the public again. He went to these places with some of his favorite disciples, and hundreds of people gathered together to listen and have their questions answered. But to everyone's surprise, the Master wouldn't talk. From the beginning to the end of the meeting–two hours–he remained absolutely silent.

Some of the seekers in the audiences were annoyed. They had come from far and wide because they had read in the newspaper and seen on posters that the Master would give a short talk, answer questions and hold a meditation. "Why won't he talk?" they asked. "He is a liar," said many, and they got disgusted. These people left the meetings early. Others stayed for the whole two hours with the hope that perhaps the Master would speak near the end, but he closed the meditations without saying anything. Some of the people in the audience felt inner joy. Some stayed only because they were afraid that if they left early others would think they weren't spiritual and couldn't meditate. So some left, some stayed with great reluctance, some stayed in order to prove themselves to others and a very few stayed with sincerity and devotion.

This went on for three or four years. There were many who criticized the Master mercilessly and embarrassed the disciples, saying, "Your Master's a liar. How do you people justify putting advertisements in the paper that he's going to give a talk, answer questions and hold meditations? He only holds meditations and we don't learn anything from them. Who can meditate for two or three hours? He's fooling us, and he's fooling himself."

Some of the close disciples were very disturbed. They pleaded with their Master again and again to give just a short talk and to answer a few questions at the end of the meditation. Finally, he agreed.

On the next occasion, the Master didn't actually forget, but he changed his mind. He kept meditating. And this time, instead of two hours, he meditated for four hours. Even his close disciples were distressed. They couldn't be angry with him, for it's a serious karmic mistake to get

angry with one's Master. But they were afraid that someone from the audience would stand up and insult him. In
their minds they prepared themselves to protect him in
case some calamity took place.

When four hours had passed and there was no sign that
the Master would either talk or close the meeting, one of
the very close disciples stood up and said, "Master, please
don't forget your promise."

The Master said thoughtfully, "My promise. Yes, I made
a promise to you people. It's my duty to give a talk. Today
my talk will be very short. I wish to say that I have given
hundreds of talks, thousands of talks. But who heard me?
Thousands of ears and thousands of eyes. My students
were the ears and the eyes of the audience—thousands and
thousands of ears and eyes. But I have failed to teach them
anything. Now I want a different type of student. My new
students will be hearts.

"I have given messages at thousands of places. These
messages entered one ear and went right out through the
other. People saw me giving talks and answering questions. For a fleeting second their eyes glimpsed something
in me and then it was gone. While I was speaking about
sublime Truth, Peace, Light and Bliss, the ears could not
receive it because the ears were already full of rumor,
doubt, jealousy, insecurity and impurity accumulated over
many years. The ears were polluted and didn't receive my
message. And the eyes did not receive my Truth, Peace,
Light and Bliss because they saw everything in their own
way. When human eyes see something beautiful, they
immediately start comparing. They say, 'How it is that he's
beautiful, his speech is beautiful, his questions and
answers are beautiful? Why can't I be the same?' Then jealousy enters. The human ear and the human eye respond

through jealousy.

"The ears and the eyes have played their role. They have proved to be unworthy students, and I couldn't teach them. Their progress has been unsatisfactory. Now I want new students and I have new students. These students are hearts, where oneness will grow–oneness with Truth, oneness with Light, oneness with inner Beauty, oneness with what God has and what God is. It is the heart-student who has the ability to identify with the Master's Wisdom, Light and Bliss. And when one heart identifies itself with the Master, it discovers its own reality: infinite Truth, Peace, Light and Bliss. The heart is the real listener; the heart is the real observer; the heart is the real student who becomes one with the Master, with the Master's realization, with the Master's vision and with the Master's eternal Light. From now on, the heart will be my only student."

*God hears
The soulful prayers of a seeker
Not only with great readiness
But also with immediate
Oneness.*

Gopal's Brother

This is a very beautiful story about Krishna, who is also called Rakhal Raja. 'Raja' means king, and 'rakhal' means cowherd–one who takes the cows to the pastures to graze. Krishna was a king and also a cowherd, so he was called Rakhal Raja, King of the Cowherds.

Once there lived an elderly man who was kind, generous and pious. He prayed to God every day. When he was very old and about to die, he said to his wife, "I'm dying. I'll leave you here on earth, but don't worry, God will take care of you."

His wife replied, "You're going to Heaven and God will take care of you there."

This couple had only one child, a little boy named Gopal. He was seven years old when his father died. The family had always lived in the forest. They were very poor and had only one cow. After Gopal's father died, his mother sold milk from the cow so that she could feed them. Although she was very poor, she was a great devotee of Lord Krishna. She prayed to Him all day and all night. She never forgot him for a moment. Her entire life was a prayer.

Gopal had reached the age where he had to begin school. The school was quite far from his home, and he had to go through the dense forest to get there. There were wild animals everywhere and he was afraid. He went to school in the morning with great fear, and when he came back in the evening, he was even more afraid because there was little light. He came home trembling and practically weeping with fear.

One day he said to his mother, "I'm not going to school anymore. I'm afraid. You have to send someone with me or I won't go."

His mother replied, "My child, I have another son, your elder brother, and tomorrow he will be with you. He stays in the deep forest and you'll find him with the cows. When you call him, he'll come play with you. He'll take you to school and bring you home again."

Gopal was very excited. He asked his mother, "What is my brother's name?"

"Rakhal Raja," said his mother.

The next morning when Gopal entered the forest on his way to school, he called out, "Rakhal Raja, Rakhal Raja, where are you?" Rakhal Raja came immediately. He looked like a real king, with a crown and a peacock feather.

So Rakhal Raja and Gopal walked together to the school. When they came near the school house, Rakhal Raja said to Gopal, "You go on. I'll come to take you home when school is over." In this way, every day Rakhal Raja took Gopal to school in the morning and brought him back home safely in the evening. Gopal was delighted with his new brother.

One day his mother asked him, "Gopal, does Rakhal Raja come to you every day?"

"Yes, he does," said Gopal.

"I told you he would. He's your elder brother," said his mother.

Rakhal Raja and Gopal were very happy together. They played games in the forest. Rakhal brought sweets and other good things for his little brother so Gopal was always happy. When he came home late his mother was not worried because Rakhal Raja was taking care of him.

A few months later, Gopal's schoolteacher lost his mother. According to Indian custom, when someone dies, a feast is held at the end of the month. So a month after the schoolteacher's mother died, there was a feast for the schoolchildren. Naturally, all the students planned to bring presents for the teacher. Gopal knew that everybody was going to bring a present for the schoolteacher, but he didn't have any money to buy one. Sadly, he asked his mother, "I want to take something to my teacher, but we're so poor. What can I do?"

"Ask Rakhal Raja," said Gopal's mother. "He'll give you something for your teacher."

In the morning, when Rakhal Raja was taking Gopal to school, Gopal said to him, "Today everyone is taking a gift to the teacher, but I am also very poor. Can you give me something?"

Rakhal Raja said, "I'm poor too, but I'll give you something." Gopal was happy to have anything that he could give his teacher.

Rakhal Raja, who was really a god, gave Gopal a small pot of sour milk, something like what we call yogurt. "Take this," he said. "Your teacher knows that you're poor. He won't mind."

Gopal was happy that at least he had something to give to his teacher. But, when he came to school, he saw that his fellow students had all brought expensive and beautiful things. So he was embarrassed and stood at the door like a thief. He didn't want anyone to see that all he had was a little sour milk in a small pot. But the teacher was kind. He took the little pot from Gopal and poured the sour milk into a large pot. He knew his servants would soon bring sour milk for the festival and that this could be added to the small potful that Gopal had brought.

When the teacher emptied the sour milk from the little pot into the big pot, he found that something miraculous had occurred. The little portion of sour milk increased in quantity. It now filled the big pot to the brim! The teacher was astonished that this tiny little amount of sour milk had become so vast.

During the festival the people who ate the sour milk Gopal brought kept exclaiming how good it was. "We've never tasted anything like this!" they said. "It's so fragrant and delightful! The flavor is delicious! It's excellent!"

The teacher said, "Gopal brought it for me. It was Gopal's gift." Then he asked Gopal, "Where did you get the pot of sour milk that you gave me?"

Gopal replied, "My Rakhal Raja gave it to me."

"Who is Rakhal Raja?" asked the teacher.

"He is my brother, my closest friend. He comes with me to school and takes me back home each day," said Gopal.

The teacher knew that Gopal had no brother. He had only one relative and that was his mother. So he asked, "Can you introduce me to your brother?"

"Yes," replied Gopal. "He is most beautiful. He has a crown, with a peacock feather in it." Gopal promised the teacher that he would take him to Rakhal Raja.

When the feast was over and everyone had gone home, Gopal took his teacher to the forest. At the usual place where he met his older brother, he cried out, "Rakhal Raja, Rakhal Raja, Rakhal Raja!" But Rakhal Raja wouldn't come to him.

He called again, "Rakhal Raja, where are you? Every day you come even when I don't call you. Now I'm crying for you and you won't come. Why are you so unkind to me? Why are you so cruel? My teacher won't believe me. He will think I am a liar. Please come, Rakhal Raja, please come." He cried and begged, but Rakhal Raja did not appear.

The teacher said, "You are a liar. Someone else gave you the milk."

Gopal shook his head and said, "No, Rakhal Raja gave it to me. I don't know why he is angry with me today. I don't know why he is not coming." And again he started calling, "Rakhal Raja, please, please, come!" But Rakhal Raja would not come.

Then Gopal and the teacher heard a voice from the forest saying, "Gopal, today I won't come. I come to you because of your mother. Your mother prays to me every day. She prays to me all the time. But your teacher does not pray to me. Why should I show my face to him? I only come to those who pray to me, those who need me."

The teacher understood who Rakhal Raja really was, and was extremely pleased that Gopal's mother was so spiritual. He could not see Lord Krishna himself, but he knew that there was someone who could see him because she prayed to him every day, and that person was Gopal's mother.

The Works of Sri Chinmoy
Music for the Heart • Books for a Lifetime

If you found inspiration in *Garden of the Soul* you might be interested in other works by Sri Chinmoy, one of the world's most dynamic figures in the world of spirituality, inspiration and self-transformation.

Books

A Child's Heart—growing up with spiritual wisdom; a guide for parents and children.

Beyond Within—essays, poetry and aphorisms on the inner life.

Death and Reincarnation—a profound work that has brought consolation and understanding to many, now in its 10th printing.

Eastern Light for the Western Mind—philosophical discussions on meditation and spiritual power.

Kundalini—a fascinating and sobering account of the yogic life force that triggers enlightenment.

Meditation—a very popular introduction to the practice of meditation.

My Life's Soul Journey—daily aphorisms and affirmations.

On Wings of Silver Dreams—questions and answers on the world of dreams.

The Master and the Disciple—a heart-warming portrait of a most unusual relationship.

Samadhi and Siddhi—a vivid and detailed first-hand account of the possibilities of human consciousness.

Yoga and the Spiritual Life—a rare insight into the philosophy of yoga and Eastern mysticism.

Cassette Tapes

Ecstasy's Trance—meditative compositions on the Indian esraj, a bowed, sitar-like instrument.

Flute Music—very haunting and rich melodies on the echo flute, reminiscent of Sri Chinmoy's Peace Concert series.

God's Compassion-Rain—unique collection of meditation music, performed on viola, bass sitar, folk drum, Chinese gong, harmonium and other international instruments.

My Heart's Promise-Sun—spontaneous and dynamic performances on the piano.

The Dance of Light—47 soft and gentle flute essays for background or meditation.

For information or to place an order call
Heart-Light Distributors at:
(206) 523-0430